Needlepoint Designs
for Traditional Furniture

Charles Blackburn

Needlepoint

VANGUARD PRESS, INC. · NEW YORK

Designs
for Traditional Furniture

Photographs by Tom Dunham

for ANNE MEACHAM

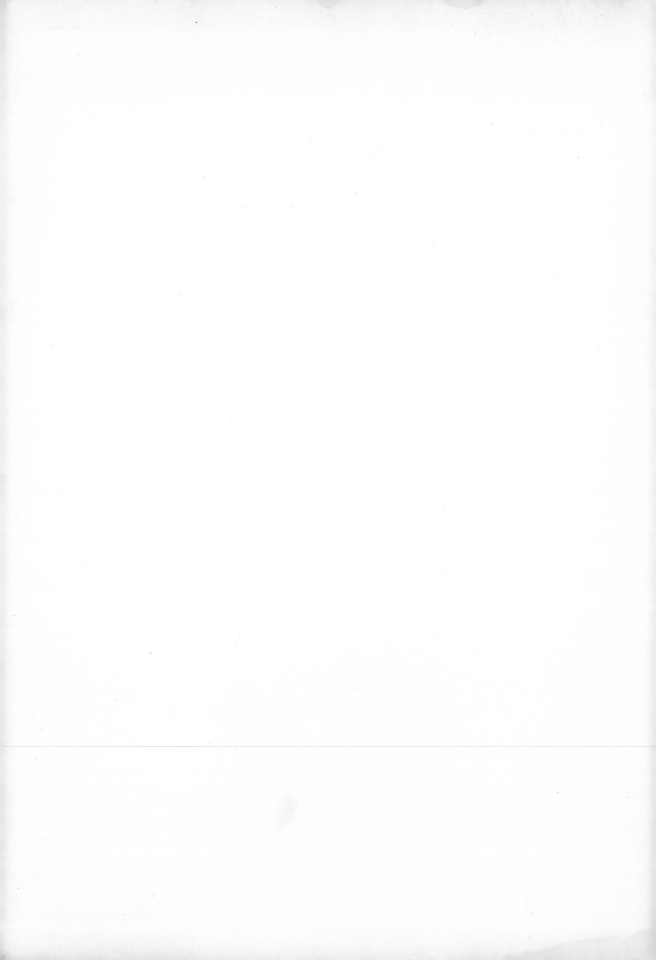

Acknowledgments

A friend in needlepoint is a friend indeed and I was fortunate in having two friends who were willing and anxious to help with the stitching of sample pieces. Janet Watson, a dancer and choreographer, plied her needle and yarn through the canvas with seemingly endless energy and enthusiasm. Paul Griffith, a writer of fiction, asked to fill in background areas, which he did rapidly and excellently. I am very grateful to them for their interest and work.

Maggie Lane, although busy with needlepoint projects of her own, found time to share ideas and opinions that were most helpful.

Margot Rosenmund is the proprietor of my own particular needlepoint haven. All the supplies for all the needlepoint pieces in this book were found at Margot Gallery, 26 West 54th Street, New York, New York, 10019. The supplies were dispensed with courtesy, friendliness, interest, and advice. Orders placed by telephone and by mail were quickly and accurately filled. In other words, my needlepoint *haven* has become a needlepoint *heaven*.

Contents

Preface

EACH month as I browse through the pages of the new issues of magazines devoted to home decorating, it seems my eye goes straight as a guided missile to one item in a pictured room that is not only a *pièce de résistance,* but also a *pièce unobtainable* — perhaps a magnificent, authentic Chippendale chair. While this furnishing is a sight to behold, it is, alas, never to "be held" by most of us.

My feeling of regret that the elegant object cannot be in my possession is tempered, however, by a thought that that chair may have been rescued from ruin at some time in the past, perhaps in its "middle age," was given an appropriate beauty treatment, and returned to a useful life in a home. Even fine eighteenth-century furniture was at one time simply "old." Tales of discoveries of some of these fabulous pieces in barnyards, junk shops, and the like are part of the "antiques" legend.

The legal definition of an antique is that it is an object of some artistic merit one hundred or more years of age. Even as I write this, many of the antiques of the year 2000, a mere twenty years away, are spending their late middle-aged years unused and unwanted simply because they are "old."

For many years I have been searching for some of these antiques of the future at flea markets, garage sales, estate auctions, used-furniture stores, and junk shops. I have even made furtive (and fruitful) explorations through piles of garbage!

I will confess here and now to an addiction to working needlepoint. What I sought at the trash and treasure markets were small pieces of furniture to receive the effects of my "habit." The true addict to canvas embroidery continually looks for fresh fields to stitch. It seemed only natural, having loaded sofas and love seats with pillows, that I would move on to stitching canvases to cover furniture seats. This book is a result of my "trips" — both to the marketplace and with canvas and yarn.

The graphed designs given in Chapter V are traditional ones. They were derived from old, antique, even ageless sources and were chosen for use with the widest possible range of furniture styles. Although rooted in classicism, none is restricted to a specific decorative period such as Victorian, Early American, or Federal.

Further consideration was given to the possibility of the use of each design on furniture of a size or shape other than the photographed sample. The finished dimensions of a piece of needlepoint worked from the charted design can be determined by you. Most often, the dimensions can be increased or decreased simply by working more or less background area.

The needlepoint pieces worked as samples and photographed on the chairs and stools shown throughout the book are small ones for the simple reason that they could be stitched and completed more rapidly than large pieces. Although this sounds so basic in premise as to be unworthy of mention, I would like to point out that a slip seat for a chair requires only one piece of worked canvas, and that piece may be attached by the needleworker with little difficulty. On the other hand, a wing chair to be covered in needlepoint will not only require the services of a professional upholsterer, but there are also a number of sizes and shapes of canvas to be stitched for such a project, and all must be completed before the chair can be upholstered.

Only you can know your level of tolerance for the amount of stitching needed for your piece of furniture. If the challenge and repetition of filling a very large piece of canvas over a long period of time appeals to you, by all means tackle the work. When your needlepoint project is finished and mounted on the furnishing you have selected, you will feel it was well worth the effort — for it will be a showpiece.

The other side of the coin is that the average needleworker often has more enthusiasm than endurance and a piece of unfinished needlepoint is . . . well, just unfinished.

Coverings for footstools, benches, slip seats, and pillows, though of modest dimensions, can also furnish a room with a show-stopping effect. And that decorative drama can be executed, if your work habits are regular, in only a few weeks.

I urge you to rescue middle-aged or old small pieces of furniture from possible obscurity. Furnish them with fresh dressings of needlepoint and you will see positive proof of the old saying, "Fine feathers make fine birds."

CHAPTER I

One Stitch at a Time

CONSIDERING the fact that needlepoint as a form of embroidery has been practiced for centuries, it is astonishing that the techniques for working it and the materials used have changed so very little. The earliest fragments of this canvas work, found in ancient tombs, show that coarse, loosely woven cotton or linen fabrics were stitched over with threads of silk, cotton, linen, or wool. What distinguishes this antique embroidery from all other types of embroidery is the even, orderly placement of the yarn or thread over a certain number of counted threads on canvas.

The materials have changed only in that they have become more refined. Canvas, wool or thread, and a needle are still the basic needs for the work. Needles, once made of bone or wood, are now made of smooth and shiny steel; evenly spun strands of wool, cotton, or silk come in a splendid spectrum of fast colors. The canvas available to us in stores is woven in a very wide range of mesh sizes, neutral colors, and widths. But the technique of working and of covering the canvas with stitches is essentially the same today as it was in the beginning. And it is still worked by hand — one stitch at a time.

The stones of the pyramids were placed there one at a time; Stonehenge was built stone by stone. Beethoven's Ninth symphony was written one note at a time. Needlepoint designs — the best and the worst — are made in just the same plodding, rewarding way: one stitch at a time.

In an age of automation and the mass production of impersonal goods, it is comforting to me to think that needlepoint, along with the weaving of baskets, can be done only by hand. While machines can knit and sew and crochet and embroider, the worker on canvas still plunges the needle with its tail of wool through the meshed fabric to build personal fantasies and illusions one stitch at a time.

After you thread a blunt-pointed needle with a length of yarn, pull some of the yarn through a piece of canvas and cover a single mesh of that sturdy fabric with a diagonal stitch slanting from lower left to upper right. You have now made the first step into the wonderful world of needlepoint.

If you place other stitches of the same kind to the right or left of the one just made, some above and below it, you will have taken a second step — this one into the infinity of design.

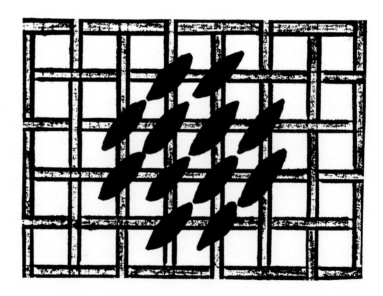

This is the challenge and the fascination of canvas embroidery: using stitches, upright or slanted, together or apart, on a rectilinear grid to create the illusion of twists and curves; or by keeping to the restrictions of box and square and angle, making geometric patterns, severe and sharp.

If you will look at a piece of needlepoint worked in the tent stitch (the slanted diagonal stitch covering a single mesh of canvas), you will see that there are no true curves in this work, only the illusion.

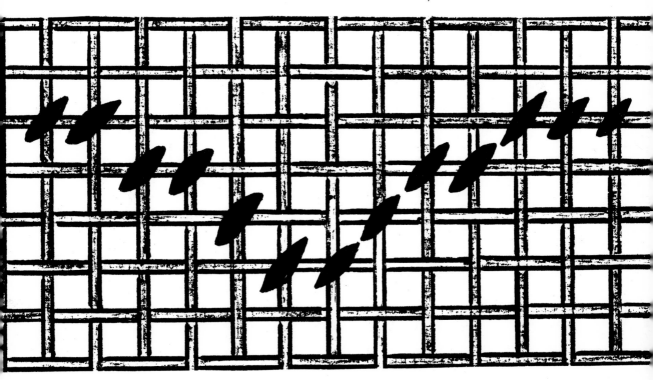

It is said that inside every fat person there is a thin one struggling to get out. In needlepoint one strives to break out of the very limited boxed and squared nature of the work. While always observing the rectilinear restrictions, we attempt to stitch spirals and tendrils, curvaceous blossoms and beasts. And, just as those who worked needlepoint many centuries ago, we make the attempt one stitch at a time.

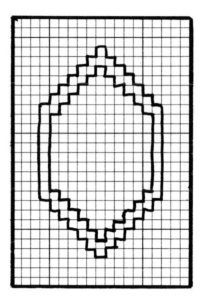

ONE STITCH MORE OR LESS

Designs for needlepoint are placed on the canvas and they emerge, take shape, and develop with one stitch more or less. A leaf shape may be stitched with a sharply defined edge.

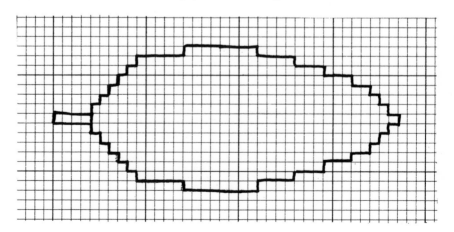

Add a stitch outside the line, subtract one inside the line and the character of the leaf begins to change.

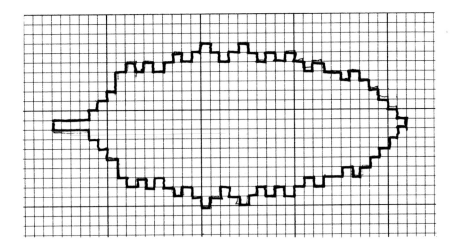

The illusion of a perfect circle worked on needlepoint canvas can be marred by one stitch more or less.

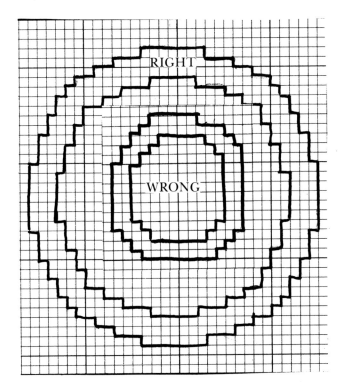

Needlepoint is illusion and reality: illusion created by one stitch more or less in building the design; reality achieved by putting the design onto the canvas one stitch at a time.

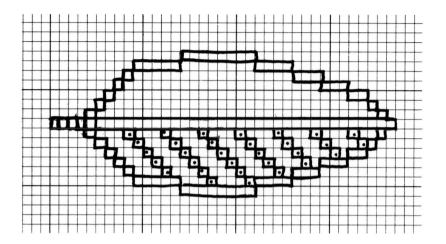

A STITCH IN TIME

As you go through this book, whether reading, looking, or working the designs, I would like to think that you will be aware that all the stitches — one at a time and one more or less — collectively form a stitch in time. Not only is needlepoint one of the oldest of the textile crafts (weaving had to come first, otherwise there would have been no canvas), but it has been practiced with thrilling effect by a host of people throughout the ages; the rich and the famous, the poor and obscure.

It *may* be that Queen Nefertiti spent lazy afternoons on the bank of the Nile decorating a canvas with stitches. Cleopatra's rewards might have been greater had she spent a few hours rendering a hieroglyphic sampler with a thoughtful saying such as "'Tis better to have loved and lost. . . ."

I *know* there have been other regal practitioners of this, therefore, noble craft. Mary, the sixteenth-century Queen of Scots, avidly, however sadly, stitched canvases in her prison cell. Another Queen Mary, wife of King George V of Great Britain, more recently and more happily, made designs in needlepoint that are now displayed in museums along with those of the doomed and imprisoned Mary.

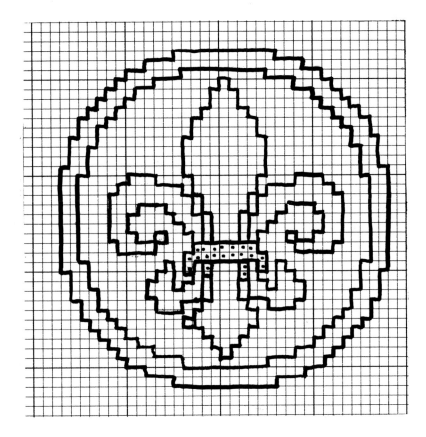

The joys of needlepoint are not restricted by station, class, or caste. As a hobby of little expense, the rewards you reap will far exceed the amount of your investment.

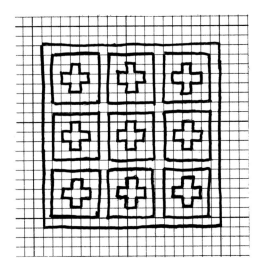

When you begin your stitch in time you should keep in mind that you will be giving, spending, and taking time to good effect, for a well-stitched piece of canvas work will endure. The life of the work may be one hundred, two hundred, or more years. After that length of time you just can't worry about it. As there are many well-preserved pieces of needlepoint dating from the sixteenth century, and those pieces were worked with materials of erratic quality (dyes were not fadeproof, nor wools mothproof), it should be encouraging to you to know that your pieces will be worked with materials superior in every way to those of the past. Dye lots are so consistent these days that in years to come, should a piece of your needlepoint need repair, the damaged area can be ripped out and replaced with the same kind of thread or yarn. The new materials will be well-blended with the old.

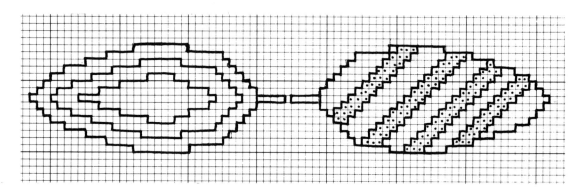

In an age when "built-in obsolescence" has become a part of the language, not to mention a part of our economic peril, needlepoint, with its timely, yet timeless qualities, seems worth the effort. It is

something worth doing, something worth keeping, and something worth passing along.

Although there are more than three hundred and fifty decorative and patterned needlepoint stitches, the mastery of the tent stitch only, the most traditional and the one most often used, can literally put the world of needlepoint into your hands. Spartan simplicity or infinite intricacy of design can come from the combined forces of fingers, needle, canvas, and yarn.

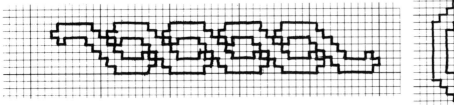 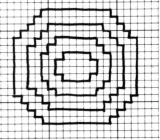

THE TIME OF YOUR LIFE

The first question usually asked of me by the uninitiated when looking at a piece of my needlepoint is "How much *time* did that take?" My standard answer, after ten years or so of guiding needles and wool through acres of canvas, is "The time of my life." This less than specific reply, perhaps unsatisfactory in terms of hours, or weeks, or months, is nonetheless accurate in essence. The time I have *given* to working needlepoint designs has given *me* the time of my life.

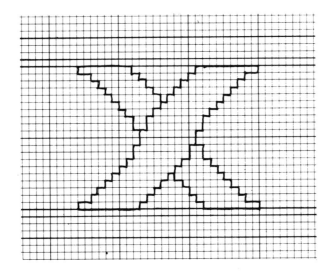

It is my hope that as you look at the graphed designs given, you will see them not only as the photographed samples suggest they be used, but also see the possibilities of combining elements of one design with those of another. A border design may become a stripe in a repeat pattern; a large motif may be lifted from the center of a square pillow and, if repeated over a large area, become upholstery fabric for a piece of furniture.

The heroine of a spicy Victorian novel, on finding herself in a pleasantly compromising situation, might resignedly exclaim, "Do with me as you will!" I would like to think that the designs included here, none racy, none compromising, will stimulate you to try combinations and concoctions other than those charted.

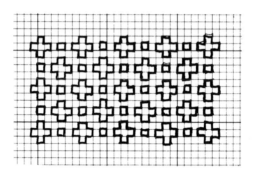

In spite of the fact that the designs were not your personal selection, when you apply them to canvas with your colors and adapt them for use in your own way, they will become yours and yours alone.

The methods and modes of working needlepoint I have included in this book are neither new nor astonishing. I have chosen a technique here, a suggestion there, a possibility elsewhere, and blended them into a way of working needlepoint satisfactory to my demands. If you follow the instructions for working needlepoint and blocking it, you will have, when all is over, a piece of canvaswork to display with pride.

And, I hope that from first stitch to last, you will have the time of *your* life.

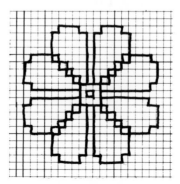

CHAPTER II

One Step at a Time

Iᶠ you are a needlepoint novice, the first step toward experiencing the raptures of the craft will be to assemble your supplies.

Pictured here are some basic needs of needlepoint: canvas, yarn, needles, scissors, thimble, crochet hook, seam ripper, and masking tape. All, with the possible exception of masking tape, will be available in a shop specializing in needlework supplies of all kinds.

The first step toward working a fine piece of needlepoint is finding a needlework shop that:

1. Carries a full line of first-rate needlepoint supplies. These will include a wide range of canvases (type, gauge, width, and color) as well as a complete selection of colors in yarns and threads suitable for canvas embroidery.
2. Has a friendly staff with a knowledge of the craft and a willingness to share its expertise.
3. Maintains a library of books on the subject — either for reference or for purchase.
4. Keeps the inventory of all the supplies current. *Nothing* is more discouraging to a worker (novice or know-it-all) anxious to begin a new project than to hear "We can order it for you. It will take about two [four] [six] weeks."

If these requirements seem stringent (for the merchandiser), there are, nonetheless, many shops across the land that meet — and sometimes exceed — them. Even shopping for a needlework shop can be interesting.

THE SUPPLIES

Canvas

All canvas for needlepoint has a *gauge number* determined by the actual number of *threads* in a linear inch. Number 12 canvas, for example, has 12 threads per inch horizontally and 12 threads vertically. The higher the number of the gauge, the finer the mesh of the canvas will be, and the more detailed the work of the design can be.

In your ideal needlepoint shop, you will find two types of canvas for sale:

Penelope is a double-mesh canvas. Each mesh consists of two pairs of parallel threads woven in such a manner that they intersect to form a mesh. The four threads may be worked over as one large stitch or separated with the tip of a needle into four small meshes.

Penelope canvas ranges in gauge from #5 through #13. The widths are from 23 inches to 72 inches. It is to be found in neutral colors such as white and ecru.

All canvas larger than #10 is of the penelope type. I use penelope

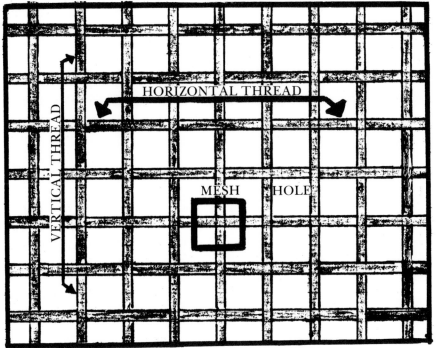

CANVAS

HORIZONTAL THREAD

VERTICAL THREAD

MESH   HOLE

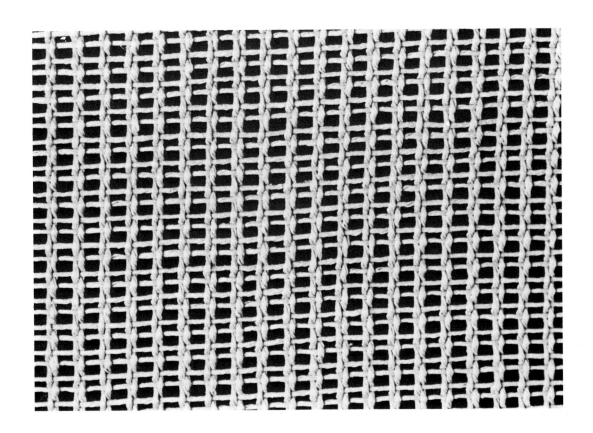

only for rugs and other large pieces of needlepoint. This type of canvas is *not* suitable for upright stitches.

Mono canvas is a single-thread type and the one I find most satisfactory for my own work. Although it is available in gauges #10 through #58(!), I find that #10, #12, and #14 are adequate for most designs. The canvas may be found in widths as narrow as 23 inches and as wide as 60 inches in white and ecru.

I recommend that you use mono canvas for your work. Buy it by the yard or half-yard in ecru, as that color is less tiring to the eyes when you work for extended periods. A 40-inch width is a good size.

The threads of the canvas will be of cotton (the most common), wool (rare), linen (expensive), silk (the finer meshes), and hemp (very large mesh sizes). The cotton threads in the best medium-gauge canvas should be thick, tightly twisted, firm, highly polished, and free of knots or thin spots. The canvas is sized to help it remain crisp and in shape as you work on it. Oil and moisture from your hands will soften the canvas somewhat as the work progresses, but the crispness may be restored easily by pressing it from time to time with a steam iron.

There are on the market today some canvases made of synthetic fibers and/or woven with permanently locked meshes. These "improvements" have not proved to be just that for me. Though this type of canvas has its followers who are loud in their praise of it, I recommend that you use a canvas woven (not locked) with natural fibers.

NEEDLES

Needles used for canvas work are blunt-pointed steel ones with large eyes. (It occurs to me that this sounds like a description of a chorus in a Wagnerian opera, even though it is an apt summation of what the needle looks like.) These needles are packaged and labeled as *tapestry needles,* although needlepoint is *not* tapestry work. Tapestries are woven on a loom; needlepoint does not require a frame or loom and is not woven.

Needles are numbered according to size: #13 is the largest and #24 is the smallest. As needles are quite inexpensive and of consistent high quality in various brand names, you should invest in several packets of them in a range of sizes. Some are packaged in assorted numbers and it would be convenient for you to have three or four of these packages in your work basket.

A size 16 needle is satisfactory for #10 canvas, size 18 for #12 and #14. The major requirements of a needle are that it should be easily threaded with the number of strands called for to cover the meshes adequately and that the needle *when threaded* should slip easily through the holes between the canvas threads.

WOOL YARN

Throughout my needlepoint life, the yarn I have limited myself to, yet never been limited *by,* is Paterna Persian Yarn, manufactured and distributed by Paternayan Brothers, New York, New York. This yarn, available in 343 colors (some have as many as eight shades in one color range) is sold in most fine needlework shops throughout the United States.

When you purchase this yarn, it will usually have been twisted into skeins weighing one ounce. Each skein will contain approximately 22 three-strand lengths of thread, each piece being approximately 64 inches long. Before using the yarn, cut these long threads in half. The 32-inch length is a good one to use for stitching. Not only is the yarn more easily separated into strands when of this length, but it will not wear thin as it is passed through the slightly abrasive canvas, as will the longer length. A shorter thread simply means you will spend a lot of time threading the needle as well as starting and finishing off threads.

Wool threads are usually referred to as "yarn." A "full" strand of Persian yarn means the triple strand as it was purchased; two strands, in needlepoint patois, means *two* of the three strands, not two three-strand lengths. The latter would be identified as two full strands of Persian yarn.

A full strand of Persian yarn is just right to cover the mesh of #10 canvas with tent stitch; two strands work well on #12 and #14.

The large black words on Paternayan's color card state that the yarns are "fast, mothproofed colors." You can depend on that.

In large black letters I would like to state: *CAUTION:* NEVER USE ANY WOOLEN YARN INTENDED FOR ANY PURPOSE OTHER THAN NEEDLEPOINT. NEVER USE SYNTHETIC YARNS FOR NEEDLEPOINT. The use of either of these materials is a *giant* step into Disaster City. The yarns will "pill," fuzz, have a flat, dull finish when stitched, and if this weren't enough to steer you away from them, regardless of the stitches used, there is a possibility that these *very* springy fibers will distort the canvas so badly that it will be impossible to block into shape. Once more, with feeling, NEVER use them.

COTTON THREAD

DMC six-strand embroidery cotton, which comes in 292 shades, has also satisfied me so completely for use in needlepoint that I have remained faithful to it. The colors are fast and the six strands are easily separated. It is available in most needlework shops in skeins of 8.7 yards. A doubled length of the thread just as it comes from the skein is perfect for covering a mesh of #12 canvas.

When using decorative stitches, their structure and texture are more clearly visible if stitched with DMC thread.

I have also used DMC's pearl cotton thread with happy results. This is a tightly twisted thread with a pearly sheen. Although it cannot be separated into strands, #3 (heavy weight) pearl cotton, when doubled, is satisfactory for use on #10 mono canvas. Number

5 (medium weight), when doubled, is fine for covering a mesh of #12 mono canvas. The color range, however, is more limited than that of the six-strand embroidery cotton.

METALLIC THREAD

About three years ago I began to use metallic thread of gold color in sparing amounts. I recall that at the time I bought the first skein of Cordonnet Metallic Thread (a French product), the salesperson advised me to pull each length of thread through a cake of beeswax before stitching with it. And also to take a tranquilizer. To be perfectly frank, while you will get about as much joy from stitching with metallic thread as you will from a mild case of the measles, the appearance of the glint of the thread in the finished product will have made the effort worthwhile. And there will be no *lasting* scars. This thread is available in gold, silver, and other colors such as red, green, copper, and purple.

THIMBLE

If you can use a thimble, and like to use one, do so. I never have and suppose I never will.

SCISSORS

Invest in a very good pair of small, sharp-pointed scissors and use them *only* for clipping ends of thread or yarn and for clipping out stitches. Use dressmaker shears for cutting canvas and large amounts of yarn.

MASKING TAPE

Masking tape is used in needlepoint to cover the raw, rough, cut edges of the canvas. The tape also keeps the canvas from raveling. Tape either one or two inches wide is fine for this binding.

CROCHET HOOK OR SEAM RIPPER

There will undoubtedly come a time, unless you are the Perfect Person, when you will have to rip out some stitches. I have ripped miles of them. Use your small sharp-pointed scissors to cut the loop of the stitch on the right side of the canvas. Pull the stitch out of the work from the wrong side. Remove the stitches just as you put them in: one stitch at a time. The tip of your needle will work for this operation, but a seam ripper or a #6 steel crochet hook will work even better.

All of the above items are the needed supplies for your work. A final word about the quality of the materials: get the best. Inferior canvas is sometimes more expensive than the best; poor quality or unsuitable wool is, in the long run, more expensive than the finest. You may think you will "save" money; and you will — at the store's cash register only. What it will *cost* you, beyond the outlay of cash for the materials, is a piece of good needlework. For no matter how fine your stitches, how glorious the design, how intricate and detailed the shading, the finished product will be inferior. Your time should be spent working with the best.

CHAPTER III

Preliminaries

WITH your newly purchased materials at hand, it is possible that you may, in an enthusiastic burst of creative energy, tackle the canvas without further preparation and create a masterpiece of stitch and design. It is also possible that you may make a mess.

Pictured here is a part of the reverse side of the first piece of needlepoint I ever stitched. It is almost an encyclopedia of errors.

The piece was started with an ocean of enthusiasm and a puddle of knowledge. There *are* two things that were done right on this piece: masking tape was used to bind one edge of the canvas and the wool chosen was intended to be used for needlepoint.

However . . . on the wrong type of canvas ("waste" canvas meant for cross-stitch embroidery), the background was executed using two kinds of tent stitch in irregular, inconsistent rows; ends of yarn were not properly or sufficiently secured; and, finally, long pieces of yarn were carried across the back of the canvas. There are other mistakes in the whole piece, all of which could have been avoided with a little preparation.

PREPARING THE CANVAS FOR WORKING

Cut your canvas to the desired size. ALWAYS add at least a two-inch margin to the finished dimensions on each of the four sides.

Bind the cut edges of the canvas with masking tape by folding the narrow width of the tape over each of the sides. If there is a selvage (there probably will be), it will not be necessary to bind that edge.

With a Mongol colored drawing pencil, mark the entire canvas between threads into squares containing ten horizontal and ten vertical threads. There will then be one hundred meshes within each square. For marking the squares, the color of the pencil should be as close as possible to the background color you intend using.

DO NOT MEASURE OR APPROXIMATE THE NUMBER OF THESE TEN THREADS; COUNT THEM.

It is essential that each large square on your canvas contain one hundred meshes, as they will then correspond exactly to the one hundred small boxes of the cross-sectioned graph paper on which the design is charted.

In the photograph of a piece of canvas that has been bound with masking tape and marked into squares, you will notice that each row of horizontal squares is identified by a letter placed in the extreme left margin. Similarly, each vertical row of squares is numbered. These letters and numbers, if placed on the graph when you have chosen a design, will make it easier for you to locate specific areas of the graphed design in the corresponding place on the marked can-

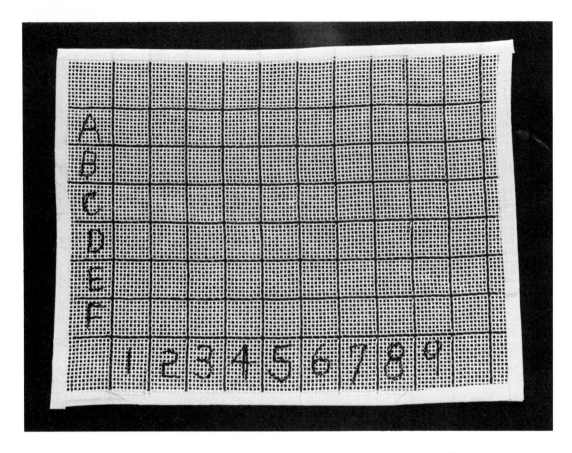

vas. Do not label the rows of squares on your canvas, however, until you have chosen and labeled the squares of the graphed design.

COUNTING FROM A GRAPH

THE TENT STITCH ON A GRAPH

When learning to count stitches from a graphed design, the very first thing you should do is look at a section of graph paper and compare that section with a piece of canvas.

Illustrated on the next page is a section of graph paper containing one hundred boxes (to your left) and a drawing of a piece of canvas containing one hundred meshes.

The one hundred *boxes* on the graph paper are established by thin, light lines. These boxes represent the one hundred *meshes* of the canvas.

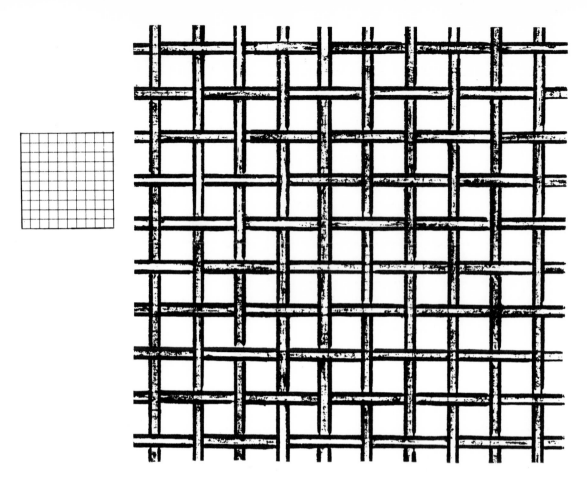

A black line drawn on the graph indicates the outside boundaries of the design; the boxes within that line represent the number of stitches necessary to make up the completed portion of the design.

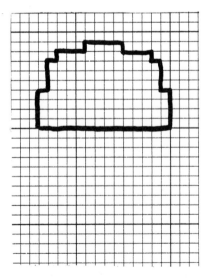

Three boxes outlined on the graph will, when the boxes are transferred to the canvas as stitches, occupy the same position on your square of one hundred canvas meshes as they do on the one hundred boxes of the graph.

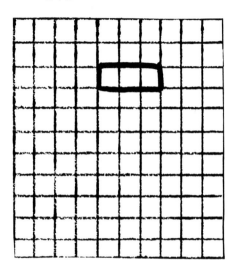

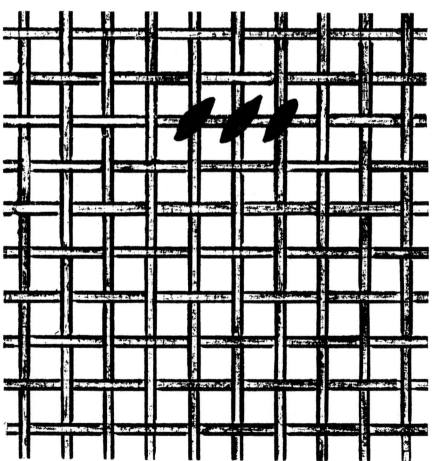

The line on the graph defining the design will follow the restrictions imposed by the angles of the boxes. As the line is drawn up or down on the graph to indicate curves or angles, it will appear as "steps." While some of the steps will include only one box per step, some will include two or more boxes.

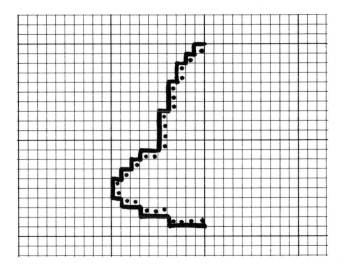

In a design intended to be worked in the tent stitch, each box on the graph stands for one of those stitches.

In most of the instructions for working the designs appearing in this book, the suggestion to "outline" the central motif appears. This does *not* mean to switch to an embroidery stitch and freely outline

The black boxes represent the boxes to be filled in on canvas with tent stitch to make an outline of the design.

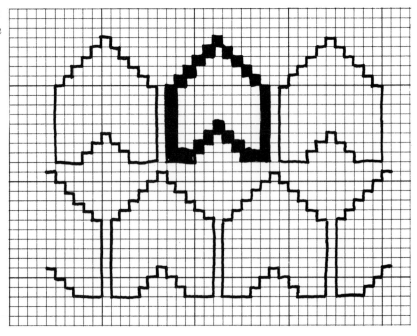

the design. It *does* mean to use the continental tent stitch (see page 51) to make a single line of stitches on your canvas. These stitches will be represented by the first row of boxes just inside the area defined by the heavy black line.

A word of caution: Some people have difficulty in learning to count from a graph because (and only because) they assume that the *lines* on the *graph* represent the *threads* of the canvas. *They do not.* Once you understand that the *boxes* on the *graph paper* represent the *meshes* of the *canvas,* you are well on your way to successful charted work.

The black squares in the boxes ...   are the X's on the meshes.

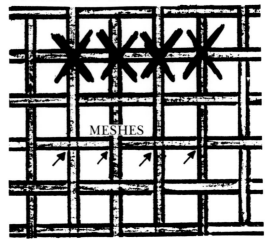

GRAPH

CANVAS

THE UPRIGHT STITCH ON A GRAPH

It's the exceptions to rules that grab you every time. The great to-do I have just made about lines not representing threads must be restricted only to the use of the slanting tent stitch.

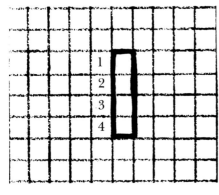

Upright stitch as indicated on a graph. The stitch covers four threads.

When upright stitches are charted on a graph, the lines of the graph paper *do* represent the vertical threads of the canvas. Boxes represent horizonal threads. As upright stitches on the canvas are placed *between* vertical threads they are sewn over horizontal threads. Thus, the graph depicts a completely accurate picture of the stitch pattern. When upright stitches are indicated by the instructions, adjust your thinking in the line/thread area.

Upright stitches, as with tent stitches, travel up or down in steps. A *4-2* step simply means that the first stitch has been sewn over four threads; the second stitch, while also sewn over four threads, has risen or dropped in placement by two threads.

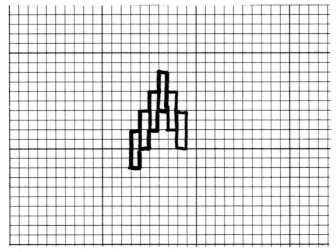

The 4-2 step charted on a graph.

The basic steps used for upright stitches to form a pattern are: 4-2, 4-1, 6-2, 6-3, and 6-1. The patterns resulting from these steps are variously known as bargello, flamestitch, Hungarian point, and counted-thread embroidery. The almost endless variations possible with the use of the steps and the combinations of them are collectively known as Florentine-stitch embroidery and it is by that name that the patterns will be referred to in this book.

Working from a graph can be more pleasant if you place the book containing the graph, or the graph paper itself, on a music stand.

A stand as elaborate as the one pictured is not essential; a collapsible one of chrome or iron will serve. Or, if a table is near your workchair, an easel-type stand will serve.

THOUGHTS ON COUNTING A DESIGN FROM A GRAPH

The first thought that comes to mind is in the form of a question: Why count from a graph when there are all those canvases already painted with designs?

My answer to myself in reply to my question is: Somewhere an anonymous designer selected a design not requiring a great amount of geometrical precision (that is, that must be counted), and painted the design in colors — usually lots of colors — that would have an appeal to the largest possible number of people and would fit in well with the décor in the largest number of homes. This is all very well and all very impersonal.

Further, the design when applied to canvas must have limits of dimension. A painted canvas design measuring 18″ by 18″ is going to remain a design with just those dimensions. It *might* be possible to squeeze out another inch or so *if* you are supplied with enough yarn of the background color.

The painted design requires some thought and consideration as you stitch, as does the counted work. A line on the painted canvas will often pass over the holes of the canvas. As the holes may not be stitched — only the threads — some time must be spent in deciding whether to make one stitch more, or one stitch less. The wrong decision can make your perfect circle become an egg.

When you work a design from a graph, not only do you have complete control over the colors and alterations (additions or deletions, major and minor) to the design, you have complete control as to the dimensions of the finished piece.

A charted design with a thread count of 144 threads by 144 threads will have the following approximate dimensions if worked on the canvas gauges listed below:

#5 canvas	28¾″ square
#7 canvas	20½″ square
#10 canvas	14½″ square
#12 canvas	12″ square
#14 canvas	10¼″ square
#24 canvas	6″ square

Shakespeare wrote, "'How often is a bush supposed a bear." Keeping in mind the wide variety of dimensions possible from a single charted design, imagine "How often may a 'bug' become a rug"!

The dimensions were arrived at by dividing the canvas *gauge number* into the *thread count* of each side of the graphed design. Thread count, of course, is the total number of threads to be worked in the design.

You should not assume that you are going to be attached to the graph from the first stitch on your canvas to the last. Careful counting of outlined areas can be done first and the filling-in can be a respite. Here are some suggestions and admonitions to make the work of counting less tedious:

1. Do not count when you are tired or your mind is distracted.
2. Counting and conversation do not mix.
3. Count carefully, don't guess. As you gain experience, you will begin to identify a series of two stitches side by side at a glance, but at the outset two stitches on the graph may appear to look like three. The graph is *never* wrong. If lines transferred to canvas do not meet, *you* have miscounted.
4. Do not count for long periods at a time.
5. When you finish a counting session, mark on the graph exactly where you finished.

CHAPTER IV

The Stitches

THE power of positive stitching is using *what* you learn *as* you learn. Your first experience in needlepoint can be, while a learning one, also a creative one: a sampler of your practice stitches.

The sampler pictured has on it examples of about 150 needle-point stitches and patterns in many kinds of thread and color shades. It was worked on from time to time over a period of two or three years. While working on other pieces that had specific purposes, such as chair seats or pillows, I kept the materials for the sampler nearby. When I wanted to see an area worked in a particular stitch or color combination I intended using on my "real" piece, I tried it first on the sampler. As I felt that the sampler, when and if finished, would be tangible evidence of a learning experience, I preferred to put my mistakes on *it* rather than running the risk of stitching errors onto my "show" canvas and having to rip them out. In time the sampler was finished, and when mounted on stretchers, it became a square yard of reference material. When I am considering the use of a particular stitch in a design, I can consult the sampler to see exactly how the stitch looks.

Many other samplers using many colors of yarn and thread have been started and may someday be finished. Not all are as formally divided into squares of 24 to 36 threads or rectangles of compatible dimensions. Some are strips of canvas, long and narrow; some are small and square; all are on canvas left over from other projects.

A sampler worked in a formal design of blocks containing 24 threads each used two colors of DMC embroidery cotton and pearl cotton in beige and tan. When mounted on stretchers, it became a small decoration for a wall.

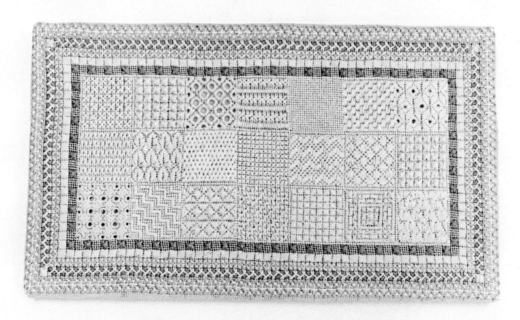

Another small sampler, the size determined by the amount of a piece of leftover canvas, was filled with stitches suitable for backgrounds other than the most-often-used tent stitch. The sampler was placed in a frame found at a flea market and has joined my "stitch library" on a wall with the other two described.

What began as a sampler of highly stylized leaf shapes outlined on a piece of canvas and filled in with decorative stitches became the covering for the slip seat of a Chippendale-style chair. The original purpose of the work was to explore the possibilities of decorative stitches and patterns within the confines of a pictorial design.

There are, then, samplers of various kinds and intents to be stitched. As all the stitches in this section should be practiced, I suggest — no, *urge* — that you make a sampler of them. I also urge you to continue making samplers of many sizes and themes even after you have become expert in making the stitches — in this way you can experiment with both color and stitch combinations.

THREADING THE NEEDLE

Grasp your needle in your right hand, the large eye upright. Holding a length of yarn in your left hand, fold a 2″-length of one end of the yarn around the eye of the needle. Use the flat surface of the needle to flatten and separate the fibers of the yarn.

Keep the now flattened fold of the yarn pinched between thumb and index finger of the left hand and remove the yarn from around the needle. Push the folded strands of wool through the needle's eye. Draw the yarn through the eye so that the once-folded end now hangs free and is about half the length of the piece of yarn falling from the other side of the needle.

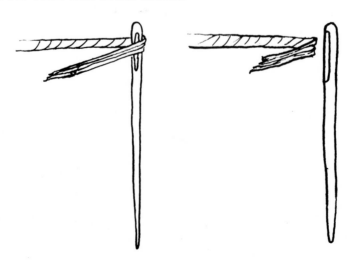

This maneuver of threading the needle may seem complicated when read; it is far less so when done. Wetting the fuzzy ends of the fibers and trying to thread the needle as with ordinary sewing thread is not satisfactory. While this method of threading may take some practice (it will), pursue the mastery of it. If your patience is gone after many tries, use a needle threader, which may be bought at your needlework shop.

STARTING AND ENDING THE FIRST STITCH

There are no knots on the back side of a piece of needlepoint. To secure an end of yarn when you take the first stitch, make a knot at one end of the yarn. Some four or five inches away from the spot where you intend to begin stitching, plunge the needle from the right side of the canvas to the wrong and pull the yarn through. The yarn end with the knot will appear on the right side of the canvas.

The knot on the right side of the canvas.

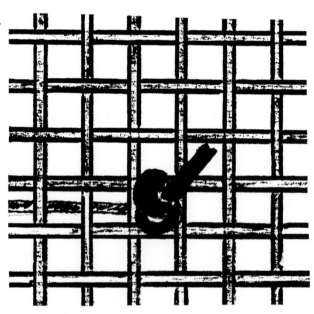

Pull the needle across the back of the canvas to the place where your first stitch will be made; bring the needle and yarn to the right side of the canvas in that spot and begin to stitch. When you have stitched the length of yarn — with the exception of three or four inches — into the canvas, complete one more stitch, leaving the needle and short length of yarn on the wrong side of the canvas. Turn the canvas over and weave the remaining yarn through the stitches just made, for a distance of 1 ½ to 2 inches; never less. Clip the rest of the yarn off and turn the canvas right side up.

Now snip off the knot on the face of the canvas; again turn the canvas to the wrong side, thread the needle with the thread just released, and weave *it* through the stitches on the reverse side of the canvas. Your first strand of yarn is completely secured.

Thread your needle with a new length of yarn, weave one end of it through the stitches, and resume your work. If you continue to stitch in the area adjacent to the first group of stitches and do so over the whole canvas, there will be no need to repeat this "waste" knot. If you begin to stitch in an area more than one inch away from a stitched area, begin as you did with the first stitch, with the knot on the face of the canvas. Do not carry lengths of thread across the back of the canvas.

THE SLANTED STITCHES

On the diagrams of the stitches shown, there are *odd* numbers to guide you as to where the needle comes through from the wrong side of the canvas to the right; *even* numbers indicate where the needle goes through the canvas to the wrong side.

THE CONTINENTAL TENT STITCH

The continental tent stitch is used mainly to outline a design, and should not be used to fill large areas, as it distorts the canvas badly. It is worked in rows from right to left or top to bottom.

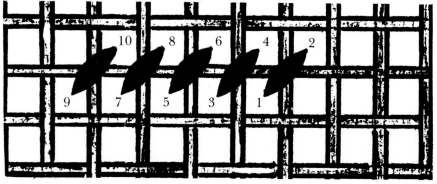

THE CONTINENTAL TENT STITCH

51

THE DIAGONAL TENT STITCH

Probably the most useful and popular stitch in needlepoint, the diagonal tent stitch is also known as the *basketweave* stitch because it forms a thick woven surface on the back of the canvas. The diagonal tent stitch distorts the canvas far less than the continental stitch and is the better to use for a tent-stitch background. Use the stitch whenever possible in a design, even in an area requiring as few as four stitches in a square.

THE DIAGONAL TENT STITCH

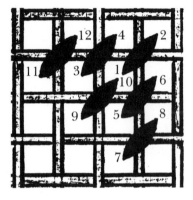

A practice square of Diagonal Tent Stitch. Begin at 1; needle goes back of canvas at 2, up at 3. When even numbers are omitted, remember the needle goes to back of canvas on even numbers, up to face of canvas on odd numbers.

The mastery of the diagonal tent stitch lies in practicing it. After you have become familiar with the *structure* of the stitches to form the basketweave on the reverse side of the canvas, you can, if you wish, learn and practice the diagonal tent stitch in its ultimate refinement: working with the grain of the canvas.

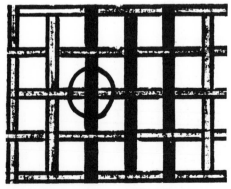

CANVAS WITH A VERTICAL GRAIN THREAD UPPERMOST

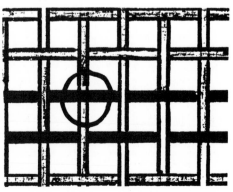

CANVAS WITH A HORIZONTAL CROSS THREAD UPPERMOST

A row of stitches moving in an *upward* diagonal direction is worked over a mesh of canvas in which a *horizontal* thread is uppermost. A row of stitches moving in a *downward* diagonal direction is worked over a mesh of canvas in which the *vertical* thread is uppermost.

Two rows of the diagonal tent stitch should never be worked in the same direction (a ridge develops). One must be very careful either to finish a thread in the middle of a row, or to work with the grain of the canvas, where a look at the thread uppermost in the mesh will guide you: upward direction — horizontal; downward direction — vertical. A simple guide of opposites.

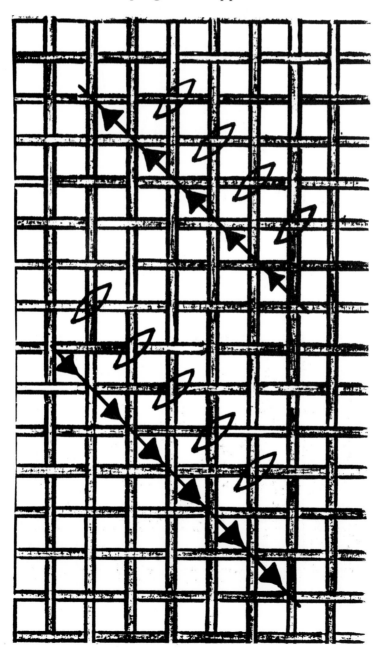

CROSS-STITCH OVER ONE MESH

All final threads of all stitches should slant in the same direction.

THE CROSS-STITCH OVER ONE MESH
may be worked one at a time or in series

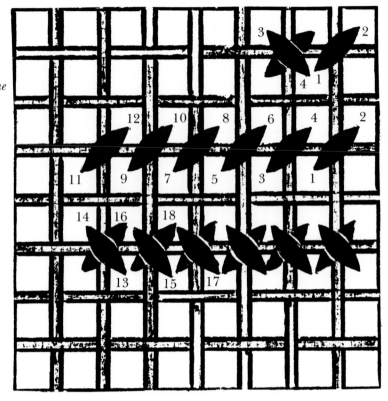

CROSS-STITCH OVER TWO MESHES

The final threads should slant in the same direction.

THE CROSS-STITCH OVER TWO MESHES

54

ELONGATED CROSS-STITCH

The elongated cross-stitch may be worked in rows with the stitches side by side, as shown, or stepped; that is, the second cross-stitch begun two threads up from the base of the first.

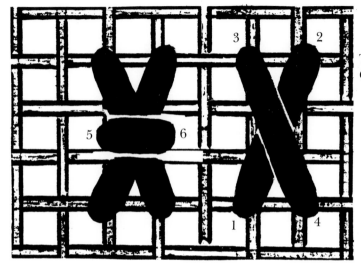

THE ELONGATED
CROSS-STITCH

THE SMYRNA CROSS-STITCH

The stitch may be worked side by side, as shown, or stepped up by one thread; all final threads should be stitched in the same direction.

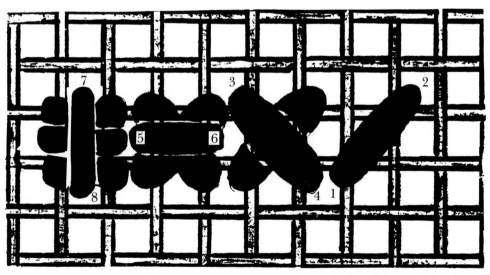

THE SMYRNA CROSS-STICH

THE DOUBLE LEVIATHAN STITCH

The stitch may be worked side by side or stepped. The last threads in a series of the stitches should be worked in the same direction.

THE CROSSED-CORNERS OR RICE STITCH

The crossed-corners stitch is effective worked in one color only or with the basic cross worked in one color and the diagonal stitches across the corners in another. The stitch may be worked side by side or stepped.

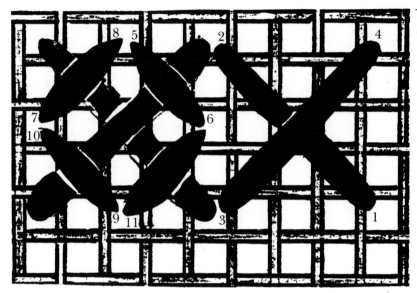

THE CROSSED CORNERS
OR RICE STITCH

THE SCOTCH STITCH

The Scotch stitch is very useful for background work; it is sturdy and works up quickly.

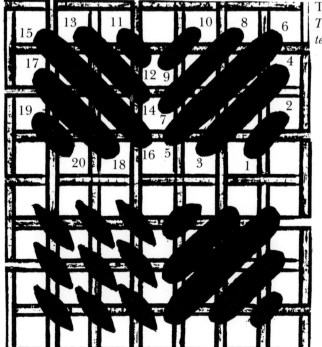

THE SCOTCH STITCH
The Scotch Stitch may be combined with tent stitch for a checkerboard effect.

THE JACQUARD STITCH

This stitch may be worked in one color only, or the long diagonal stitch worked in one color, the shorter ones in another.

THE JACQUARD STITCH

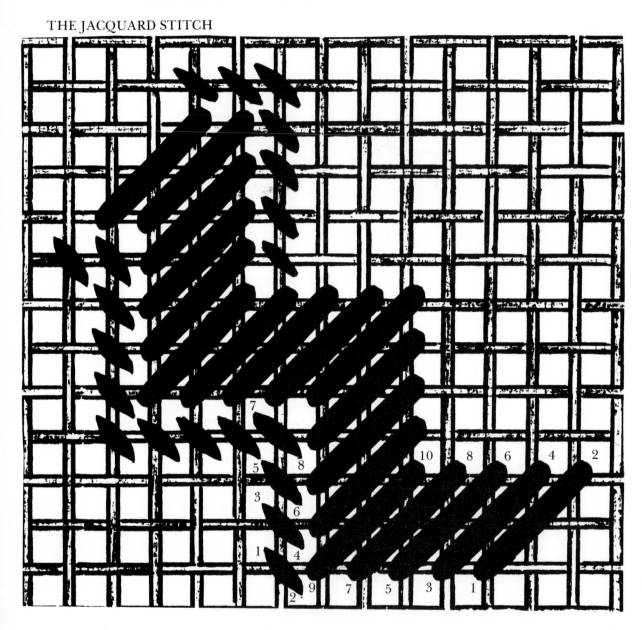

THE UPRIGHT STITCHES

Upright Stitch over Two

This is traditionaly called the upright Gobelin stitch, but I prefer the descriptive title I have given it. It may also be worked over four threads, in which case it would be called the Upright Stitch over Four.

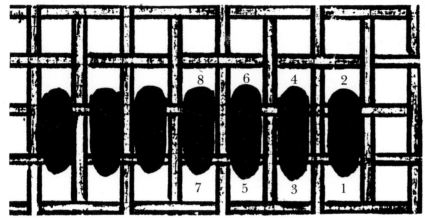

UPRIGHT STITCH OVER TWO THREADS OR GOBELIN STITCH
may be worked also over three or more threads

Old Hungarian Stitch

I sometimes refer to this as the 2-4-2 stitch because this is its structure.

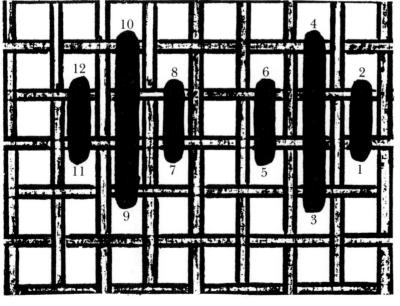

THE OLD HUNGARIAN STITCH

59

Florentine Stitch: 4-1 Step

The pattern resulting from a group of these stitches is, of course, only one of the many possible patterns, as peaks and valleys of the design have stitches added or subtracted.

THE FLORENTINE STITCH:
4-1 STEP

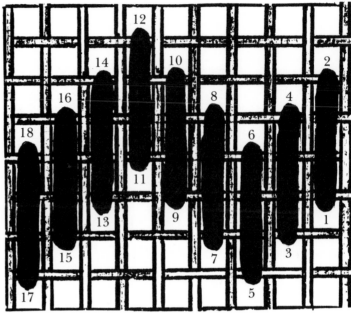

Florentine Stitch: 4-2 *(Bargello)*

This is the most common of the Florentine steps and the basic stitch and step of flamestitch patterns.

THE FLORENTINE STITCH:
4-2 STEP

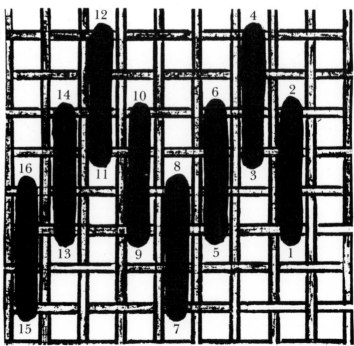

BRICK STITCH OVER TWO

An excellent background stitch.

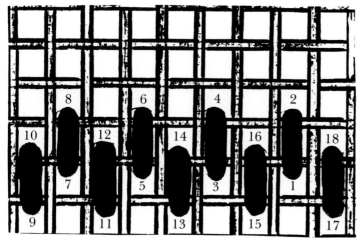

THE BRICK STITCH
OVER TWO THREADS

BRICK STITCH OVER FOUR

Good for backgrounds if the canvas gauge is not large.

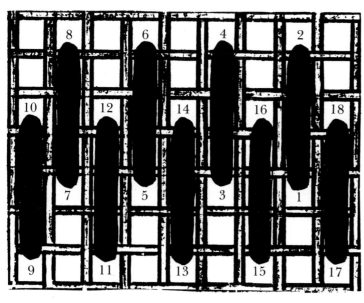

THE BRICK STITCH
OVER FOUR THREADS

Double Brick Stitch over Four

An effective background stitch, it may also be worked as Double Brick Stitch over Two.

THE DOUBLE
BRICK STITCH
OVER FOUR THREADS
*may also be worked over two
threads*

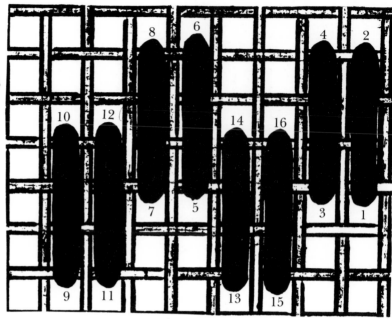

HYBRIDS

Hybrids are stitches combining slanted and upright stitches.

Leaf Stitch

This is, as you will see in the designs, a personal favorite of mine. It is durable, rapidly executed, and as effective for backgrounds as it is for filling in areas of a design.

Diamond Eyelet Stitch

If this stitch is sewn with little tension, there will be a solid look; if the thread is pulled tightly as each is stitched into the canvas, a hole will appear in the center of the finished stitch.

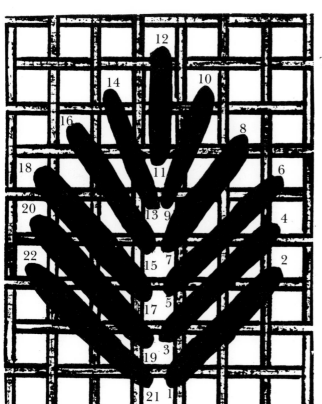

THE LEAF STITCH

THE DIAMOND EYELET STITCH

All threads return to the back of the canvas through the center hole.

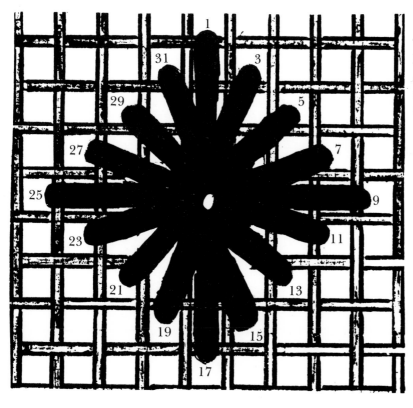

While the basic structure of the eyelet stitch does not change, the number of threads and meshes do when the stitch is made as a round eyelet, half round, or square.

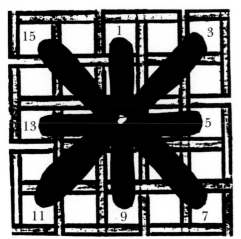

SQUARE EYELET   *EYELET VARIATIONS*   HALF-ROUND EYELET

The Ribbed Wheel (*Chrysanthemum*)

This stitch makes a very thick textured surface on top of the canvas. But while it is sturdy, it may be subject to snagging.

WHIPPING THE SPOKES
OF THE WHEEL

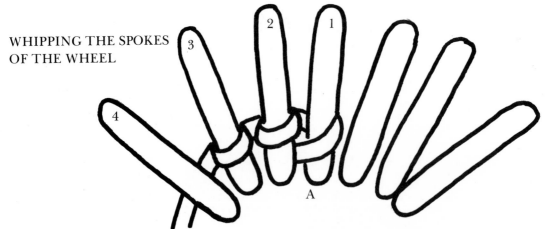

The needle and thread come to the top of the canvas at A. Thread passes across the top of long stitch 1, passes under *stitches 1 and 2 (under the* stitch, *not under the canvas). The thread passes across stitch 2, goes under 2 and 3, around 3, under 3 and 4, and so on around each spoke of the wheel.*

Continue in this whipping action until each of the long stitches is packed tightly with the whipped threads. If you need to finish off a piece of yarn, pull it to the back side of the canvas, finish it off, and begin again where you left off.

64

THE RIBBED WHEEL
The center threads are worked in the Double Leviathan Stitch.

Except for tent stitches on canvas gauges as noted previously, there are no satisfactory rules for determining the number of strands of thread to use for decorative stitches. Simple upright stitches, such as the Florentine stitch, usually require more strands than a stitch crossed or stacked up with several crosses, such as the double Leviathan stitch. This is another good reason for working a sampler as you stitch a project: to determine how many strands are needed to cover the canvas adequately.

When using the tent stitch, do not use *more* strands than cover well. Too many strands will cause the canvas threads to be pushed together more closely row after row. Within a short space the threads will have become so close together that it will be impossible for the needle to slip between them. Two options are then open to you — rip out all the stitches or throw the piece out.

If you are considering stitches for use on canvas as an upholstery fabric, don't reject the long, upright stitches as being fragile or more subject to wear than others. Perhaps the most famous chairs bearing needlepointed upholstery are the Bargello chairs in the museum of that name in Florence. The chair coverings are embroidered with long, upright stitches and have survived from the eighteenth century, as have many, many pieces of flamestitch of the same period. It stands to reason that upholstery of the same design worked with modern materials will survive for as long a time or even longer. Florentine embroidery for upholstery, however, should not be worked on a canvas gauge coarser than #12.

CHAPTER V

The Designs

It occurred to me that this section might be called *e unum pluribus* — out of one, many — as that phrase, a reversal of our country's motto, aptly describes many of the designs. It is certain that one's entire life could be spent exploring the possibilities of pattern using the Florentine stitch steps alone. In a flamestitch pattern, for instance, the pattern changes as the number of stitches in the lines forming the peaks and valleys of the flames are varied. Even the same pattern worked on two different canvases, using the same colors for both, will appear to be two completely different designs if the sequence of colors is changed on the second one. A repeat pattern when worked with a background color of white and the repeated motif in green will appear to be quite different if the colors are reversed. In design, this is called a "counterchange."

The colors you choose for the design will influence the style of the piece. The Bee and Rosette design (page 136), with its sophisticated palette of cream, brown, and metallic gold, can, if worked in red, blue, and yellow, become more casual in character. The "sting" of the bees and of the colors will depend on your choice of those colors. The true hues as found on a live bee may limit your work; and as insects, when stitched on canvas, are not *real*, my opinion is that the colors used to do not have to be literal. It is said that all cats are gray

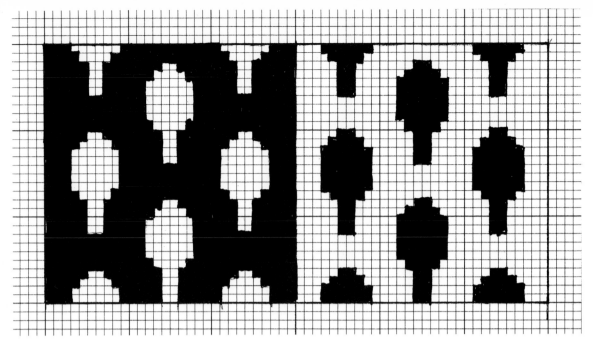

A COUNTERCHANGE

in the dark; it is possible that a white Persian cat, seen by the light of an autumn moon, may be lavender! While it is admirable to see things as they *are,* it is creative to see them as you wish them to be.

Be sure, when you select colors of yarn and thread, that you truly *like* the colors, the background color in particular. It is possible you will be stitching with them for some time. Be aware, also, that thread when stitched onto the canvas appears slightly darker than in the skein.

Very bright, very clear colors seem to be more tiring to the eyes as one works with them for a long period of time. They also have a tendency to seem static in any light. Colors made of two or more shades appear to change with the changing light. If you find this refreshing — and I do — you will choose your colors only after you have seen them in natural as well as in artificial light. Then you will love them in December as you did in May.

It is my belief that needlepoint as a decorative, functional, sturdy textile can have a wide range of uses in the home. My choices so far have included using it for pillows, rugs, decorative wall pieces, and upholstery.

Those who protect their needlepoint-in-progress with layers of tissue paper wrappings, *that* packaging encased in a plastic bag, and the whole bandaged shebang secreted in a box like a "craft mummy", should look at the work and see that they are creating a piece of fabric of great durability. It should be remembered that the base of the fabric, a sturdy canvas, can hardly be torn; and that the canvas will eventually be like the middle layer of a needlepoint sandwich — completely covered on both sides with an equally durable material — perhaps wool. I have in use a flamestitch rug that has outlasted three bathmats in a bathroom. It has been washed (!) many, many times, and even after eight years shows no signs of wear.

I think my further interest in needlepoint as fabric was triggered by something I witnessed in a needlework shop some ten years ago.

A customer in the shop was buying a couple of yards of natural-colored canvas and an equal number of *pounds* of black yarn. When the client left the store with her purchases, I asked the owner if he knew for what purpose all that background yarn was intended. He rolled his eyes to the ceiling, heaved a weary sigh, and said, "Background? She is going to do the seats and backs of her chrome and plastic dinette chairs . . . in SOLID BLACK NEEDLEPOINT!"

My immediate reaction was a unique combination of horror and admiration. Horror at the effort to be expended when, in this case, real fabric would have been more practical and more suitable; admiration for someone who must have the highest threshold of boredom since Penelope (for whom that type of canvas is named).

Well, each to his own taste, as the old woman said as she kissed the cow.

And so, on to the charted designs. Work them as you find them, alter them, add to them, take from them, and make them your own.

Designs graphed here for your use will have a set of instructions listing the kind of thread used in the sample piece and the color numbers. A thread count of those designs with a central motif will also be given along with the gauge canvas used. Actual dimensions of the sample piece will be furnished when the design has a border enclosing it. Dotted or shaded areas indicate a change in color.

Designs using the Florentine stitch in repeating patterns will not have a thread count furnished, as these designs are intended to be used as fabric and its thread count will be determined by the size of the piece of furniture on which it is intended to be used. A suggested sequence of colors, however, will be included.

SAW-TOOTH REPEAT (COLOR PLATE 12)

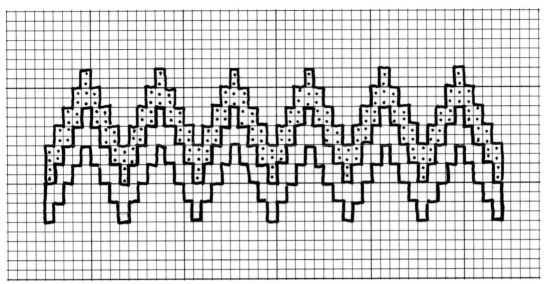

Dotted row indicates second color.

Suggestions for working:

The sample piece is worked on #12 mono canvas using the Florentine stitch, 4-2 step.

Four strands of Persian yarn (one full strand plus one added) are used. The colors are stitched in the following sequence: navy blue 365, lightest orange 454, lighter orange 444, darker orange 434, darkest orange 424, 434, 444, 454, a repeat of blue 365.

This sequence of colors is repeated over the entire working area of the canvas. It will not be necessary to mark the canvas into squares when working the Florentine stitch patterns.

When beginning work on this design, first stitch in the dark line of navy blue on the horizontal center line of the canvas. Rows to be worked above and below this first line will be a repeat of the pattern thus established. It will not be necessary to refer to the graph after the first row is put on canvas.

FLAMESTITCH REPEAT (COLOR PLATE 6)

Suggestions for working:

The sample piece is worked on #12 mono canvas using the Florentine stitch, 4-2 step.

Four strands of Persian yarn were used.

The colors are stitched in the following sequence: white 005, followed by seven graduated shades of gold, 040 being the lightest, followed by 438, 437, 442, 441, 440, to the darkest, 427. Following the line of darkest gold 427, the colors are reversed: 440, 441, 442, 437, 438, 040, white 005. This "water-color" effect in gold is followed by seven rows of blues in the following sequence: 395 (lightest), 386, 385, 330 (darkest), 385, 386, 395, white 005. Repeat the gold colors in the same sequence as before.

Begin the pattern on the vertical center line of your canvas. Place the first stitch of the highest peak at this point. Work to the left of the center line and stitch, then complete the right side of the line. The first line of pattern is stitched with white 005, rows above and below this line follow the sequence outlined above. As with the sawtooth design, once the first line is put on canvas, there will be no need to refer to the graph.

The boxing strip for the chair as shown in color plate 6 uses only the colors in the gold range. The first line of stitching is gold 427 and shades from that deep color to the lightest on either side of the line as graphed.

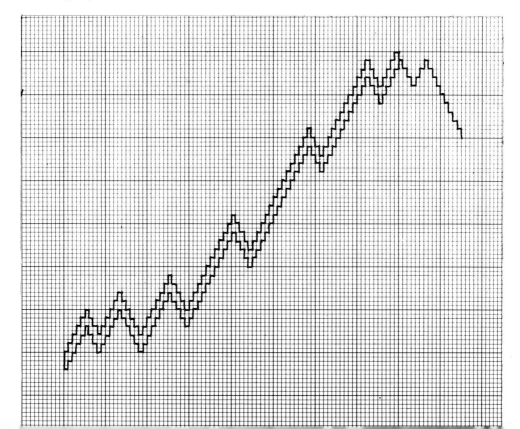

FLAME STITCH REPEAT

If more pattern is needed for the width you have chosen, you may add by reversing the pattern as shown, or add to it with your own peaks and valleys.

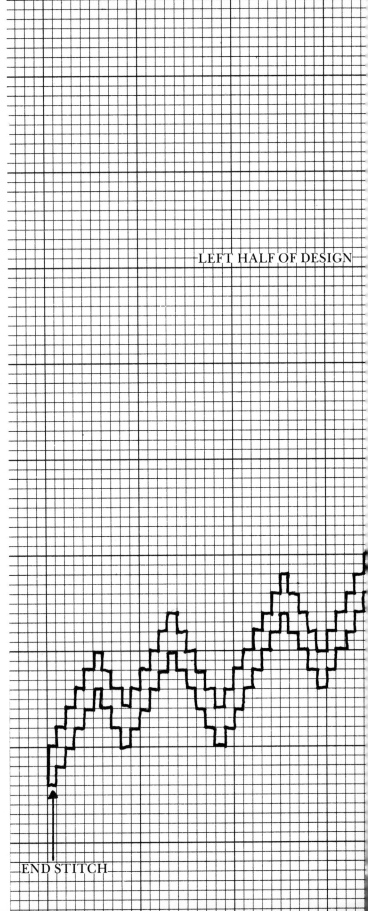

LEFT HALF OF DESIGN

END STITCH

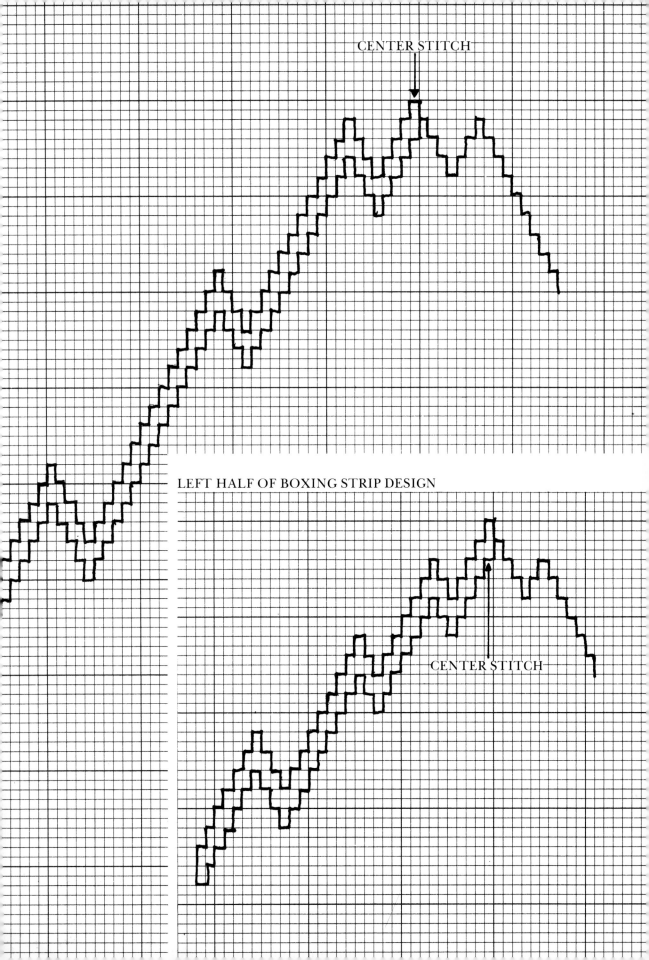

CENTER STITCH

LEFT HALF OF BOXING STRIP DESIGN

CENTER STITCH

CARNATION REPEAT (COLOR PLATE 1)

Suggestions for working:

The sample piece is worked on #12 mono canvas, using the Florentine stitch, 4-2 step.

Four strands of Persian yarn are used in the following colors: white 005, pink (darkest) 821, slightly lighter 827, lighter 828, lightest 831; green 505.

The shape of the carnation is outlined in white 005. The calyx of

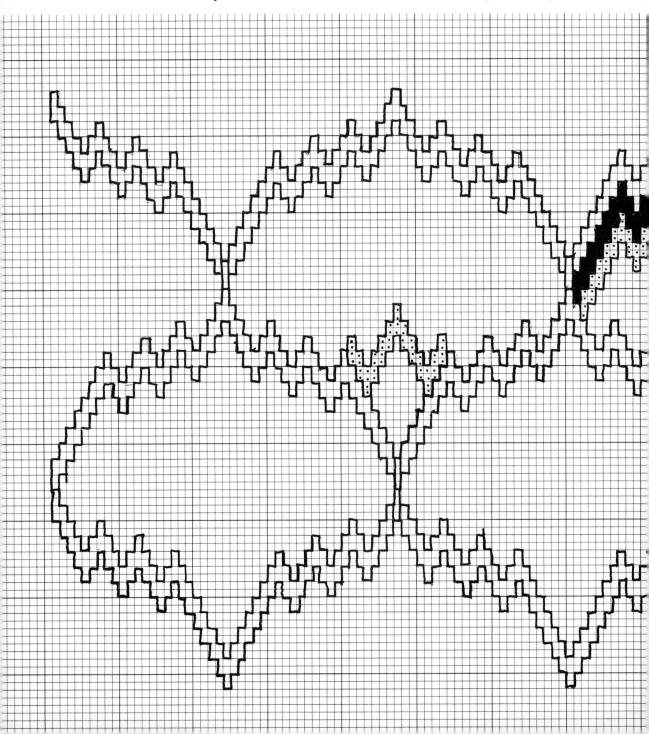

the flower, the dotted diamond shape on the graph, is worked in green 505.

Below the white line at the top of the carnation, stitch with pink colors in the following order: 821 (darkest), 827,828, 831, 828, 831.

You will notice, as you work the white outlines of the carnations, that the second line of the pattern which forms the tops of the flowers is identical to the first in count; the difference is that the peak forming one side of the carnation becomes, on the second row, the center top of it.

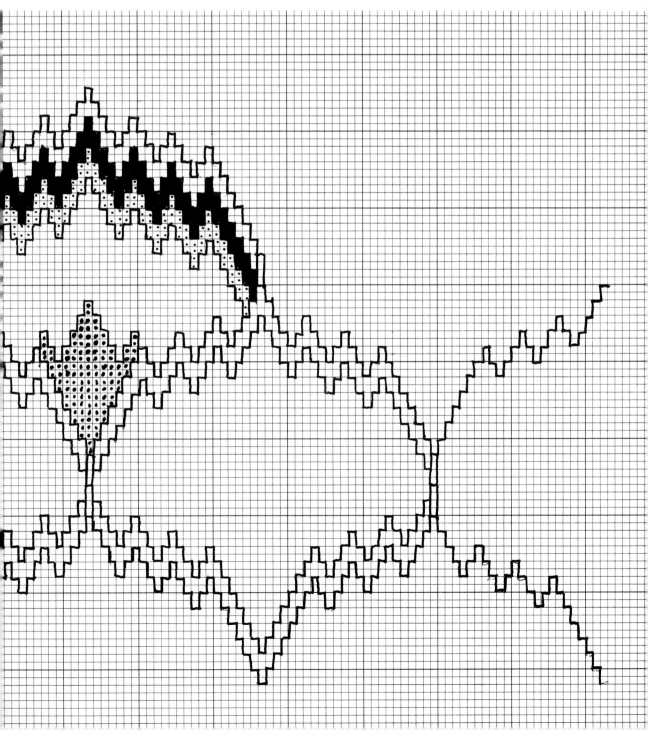

THE RIBBON REPEAT (COLOR PLATE 4)

Suggestions for working:

The sample piece is worked on #14 canvas of the mono type, using a full strand of Persian yarn for the Florentine stitch and two strands for the Smyrna, double Leviathan, and tent stitches. The thread count of the width of the strips is 24 threads.

The following colors are used: orange 424 (darkest), 434 (lighter), 444 (lightest), brown 104, cream 015.

Work first all stripes of tent stitch as follows: Double row of tent stitches on the left with orange 424; single rows of tent stitches outlining the stripe containing Smyrna stitches (the next row to the right) are worked in brown 104. Work Smyrna stitches in cream 015; fill in between with tent stitches of brown 104. The next stripe-within-the-stripe is defined with a single row of tent stitches worked in orange 424. Skip *six* threads and work another single row of tent stitches. Fill in the vacant six threads just made with Floren-

Appliqué ribbon here.

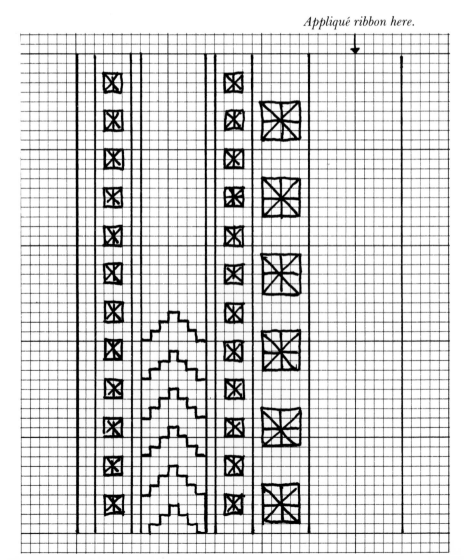

tine stitches, 4-1 step. The first and last stitches within the area will share the holes of the canvas with the tent stitches. The next row of Smyrna stitches is worked the same way as the first one: one row of brown 104 worked in the tent stitch, skip two threads, a second row of 104. Make Smyrna stitches with cream 015, fill in between with brown 104, using the tent stitch. Next, using the medium orange 434, stitch a single row of tent stitches, skip four threads, work another row of the same color. Stitch double Leviathan stitches in cream 015. Fill in with tent stitches, using orange 434.

As this repeat pattern uses lengths of ribbon in between the stripes, you must obtain the ribbon before proceeding further. In the sample piece, brown velvet ribbon ¾″ wide is used. It is necessary to omit only ten threads of stitching to accommodate the width. Try the ribbon you plan on using, count the number of threads the ribbon covers, and do not stitch them.

I suggest working all the needlepoint stripes before applying the ribbon to the canvas. The patterned stripe may be reversed in order or you may continue the original pattern. It is also possible to place a length of ribbon between each of the stitched stripes-within-a-stripe.

Apply the ribbon to the canvas, using regular sewing thread and needle; use a tent-type stitch to appy it, catching only the edge of the ribbon to the mesh of the canvas.

PATTERNED STRIPES (COLOR PLATE 7)

These patterned stripes were designed to be used together or separately or in combinations with stripes from the design preceding this. All are derived from seventeenth-century fabrics.

Suggestions for working:
The sample piece is worked on #14 canvas of the mono type. The colors of Persian wool used are: taupe 136 (lightest), 134 (medium), 124 (darkest). Cordonnet Metallic threads in gold and silver are also used. A full strand of Persian yarn is used for the Florentine stitch, 4-1 step; a double strand of the metallic for the 2-1 step, as well as Smyrna and double Leviathan stitches worked with metallic thread.

The Chevron stripe is worked with wool used on the longer stitches, the colors arranged in the following sequence: taupe 124,

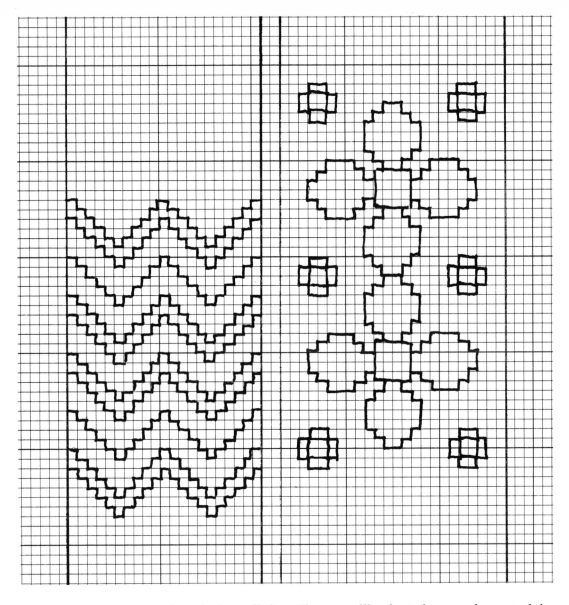

134, 136 — dark to light. The metallic threads are alternated in colors: gold, silver, gold.

The Leaf and Bead stripe uses gold metallic in the double Leviathan stitch for the center of the leaf motif. Leaf stitches are worked in taupe 136. The beads between the horizontal leaves are silver metallic Smyrna stitches with two tent stitches on each of the four sides worked in taupe 136. The background is tent stitch, darker taupe 134, two strands.

The thread count of each of the stripes is 24 threads in width. In the Leaf and Bead stripe, some of the tent stitches will share holes with the decorative stitches.

PERSIAN MEDALLION (COLOR PLATE 11)

The sample piece was worked on #12 canvas, using the following colors: Persian yarn in red 952, cream 015, and brown 124. The metallic is Cordonnet gold.

Thread count of the medallion is 118 by 118.

Suggestions for working:

Using cream 015, outline and then fill in the border of the small design in the center of the medallion. Use tent stitch.

On the outside of this border, outline the design with a single row of tent stitches, using gold metallic. Work a single outline row of tent stitch outside the metallic, using brown 124.

Outline and fill in the border of the larger design, using cream 015. Place a single row of tent stitches in brown 124 on either side of this border.

Fill the center of the smaller design with a checkerboard pattern of double Leviathan stitches in red 952 and gold metallic. In areas near the inside of the border, where there are not enough threads to accomodate the double Leviathan stitch, use Smyrna cross-stitches or tent stitches to continue the checkboard effect.

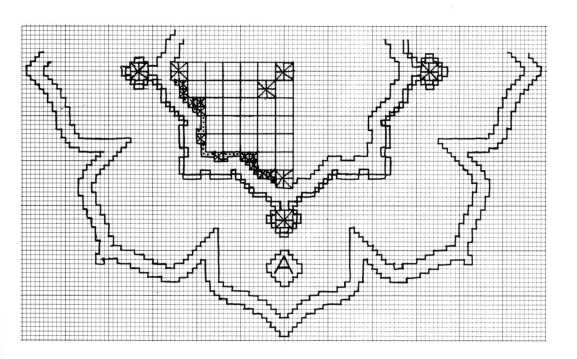

Place a double Leviathan stitch of metallic thread in the four projections of the center motif.

Fill in the large area surrounding the center motif with Diamond

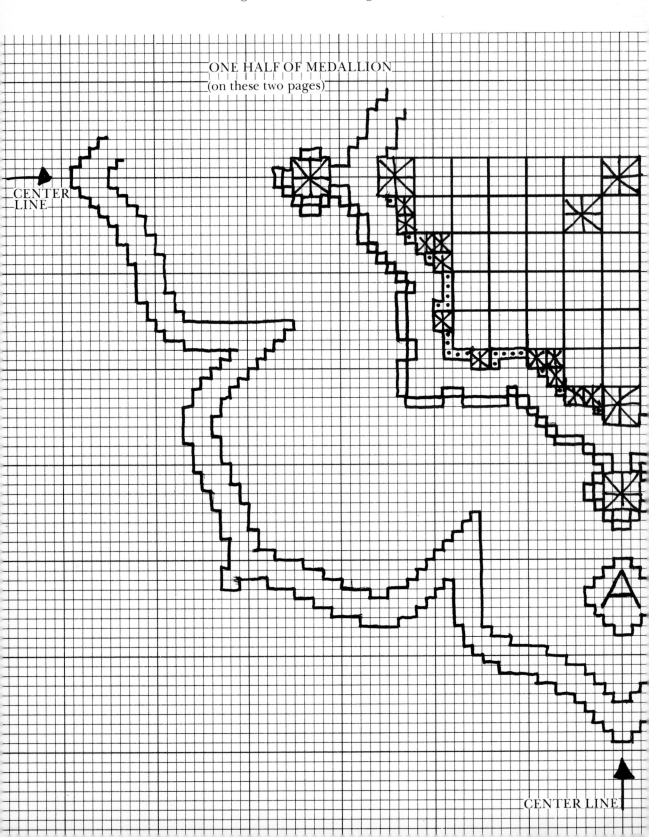

eye stitch, using cream 015. Begin stitching at the place indicated on the graph marked with an A.

The background was worked in the Old Hungarian stitch with red 952.

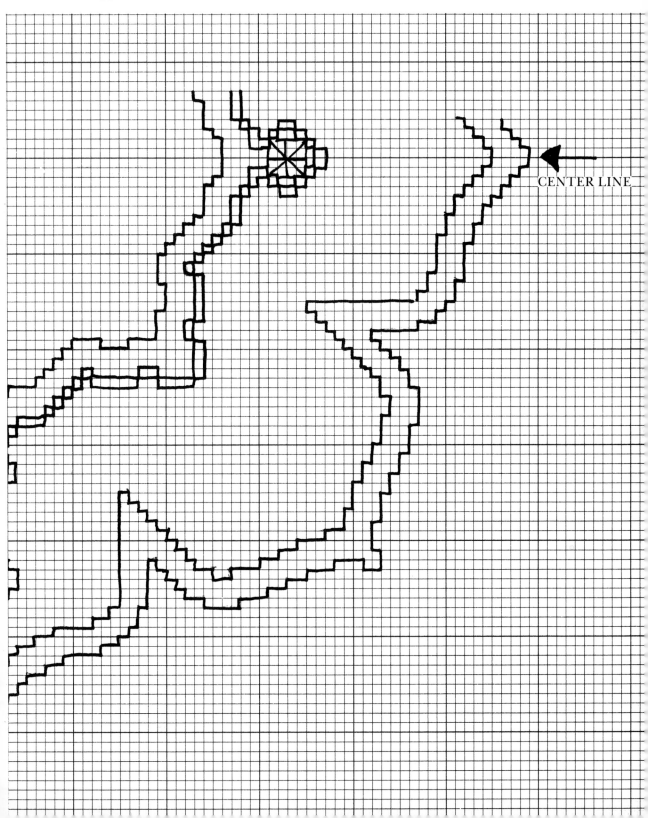

CENTER LINE

PINE-CONE MEDALLION

The Pine-cone Medallion has an outside border almost identical to the Persian Medallion.

The sample is worked on #8 penelope canvas. The thread count is 119 by 119. (The axis of the Persian Medallion is *between* threads; because of the even-numbered thread count, the center line of the Pine-cone design is on a *thread*.) Persian yarn in the following colors was used: red 952, white 005, dark blue 330, medium blue 386, light blue 395.

Suggestions for working:

Mark the canvas into squares.

Using the tent stitch, outline and fill in the outside border with red 952.

Outline and fill in the circular border in the center of the design with red 952.

Stitch single lines of Pine-cone motifs in tent stitches, using dark blue 330. Smyrna stitches on the pine cone are worked in medium blue 386. Squares between the Smyrna stitches are tent stitches in blue 330. Dotted blocks on the cone are worked in tent stitches, using blue 386.

The leaves on the petals of the medallion between those containing the pine cones are worked in the three shades of blue: the large scrolled leaf nearest the center uses dark blue 330; the middle one, medium blue 386; the tip, 395.

The background is worked in tent stitches, using red 952 for the latticework, white 005 for the stitches between the lattice pattern.

The design would benefit from an outline of blue 330, worked in a single row around the outside of the medallion.

The pine cone as adapted for a repeat pattern makes attractive fabric for upholstery.

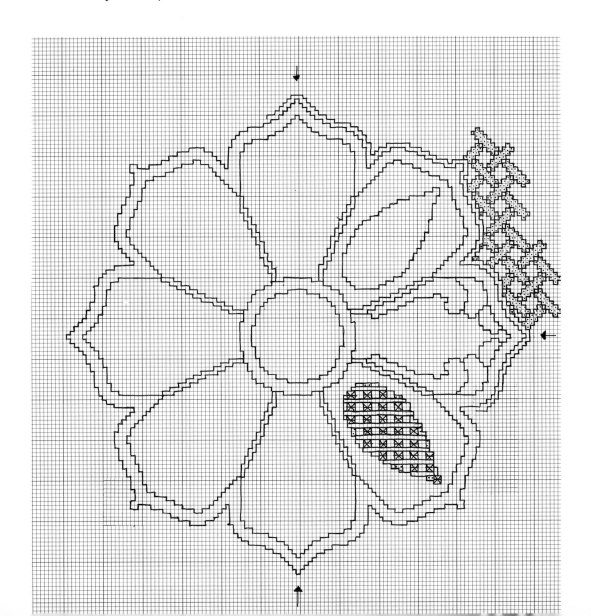

PINE-CONE
MEDALLION

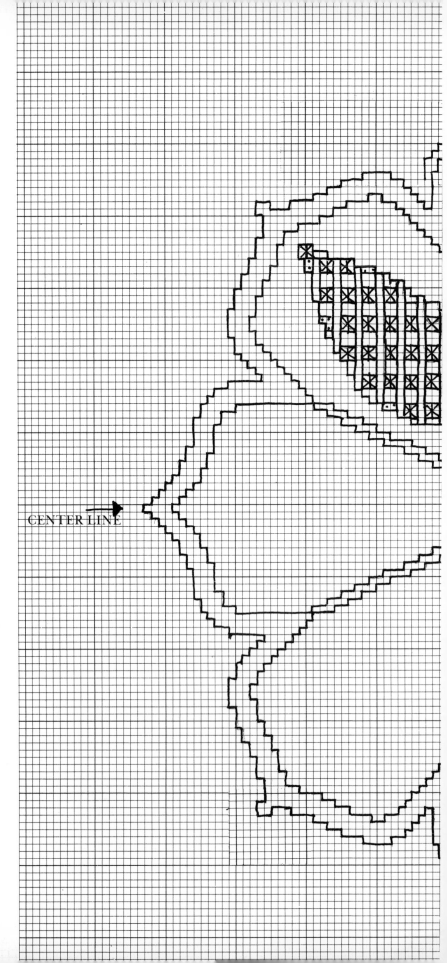

CENTER LINE

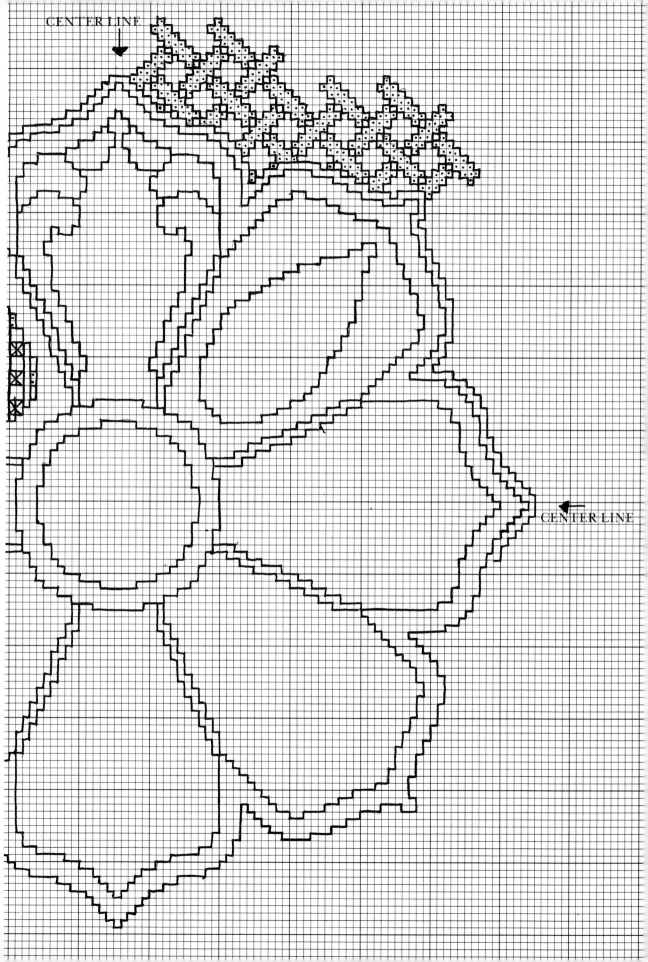

CENTER LINE

CENTER LINE

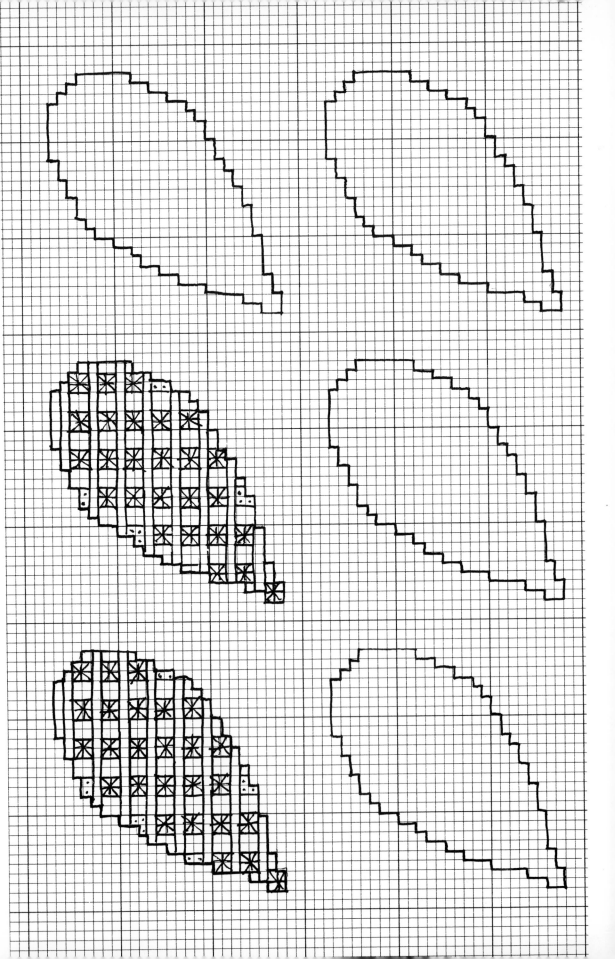

LIONS (COLOR PLATE 2)

The sample piece is worked as a pillow on #12 canvas, using Persian yarn in the following colors: white 005, dark blue 365, medium dark blue 330, lighter blue 385, lightest blue 386.

The thread count of the lions is 53 by 92.

Suggestions for working:

Outline and fill in with tent stitches the lion's face, using blue 386. The eye is a Smyrna stitch in blue 365. The two stitches above and the three below the eye are blue 330, as are the three stitches at the mouth. Work the tongue in blue 365. Outline and fill in the mane with blue 330. The body of the lion and the legs in the foreground are worked in blue 386. Pads on the feet are in Smyrna stitches, blue 386. Claws (dotted on the graph) are blue 365. The other two legs are worked in blue 330 as are the pads of the feet. Claws are blue 365. The shorter portion of the tail is worked in blue 385, the other in blue 386. Background is tent stitch and the color is white 005.

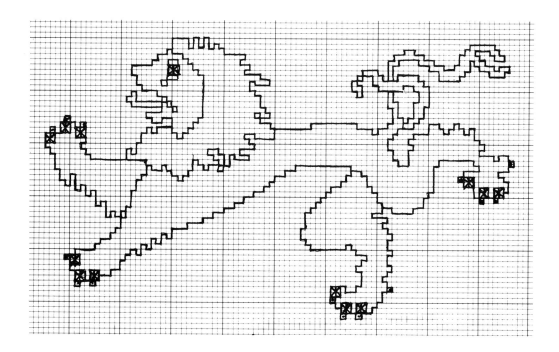

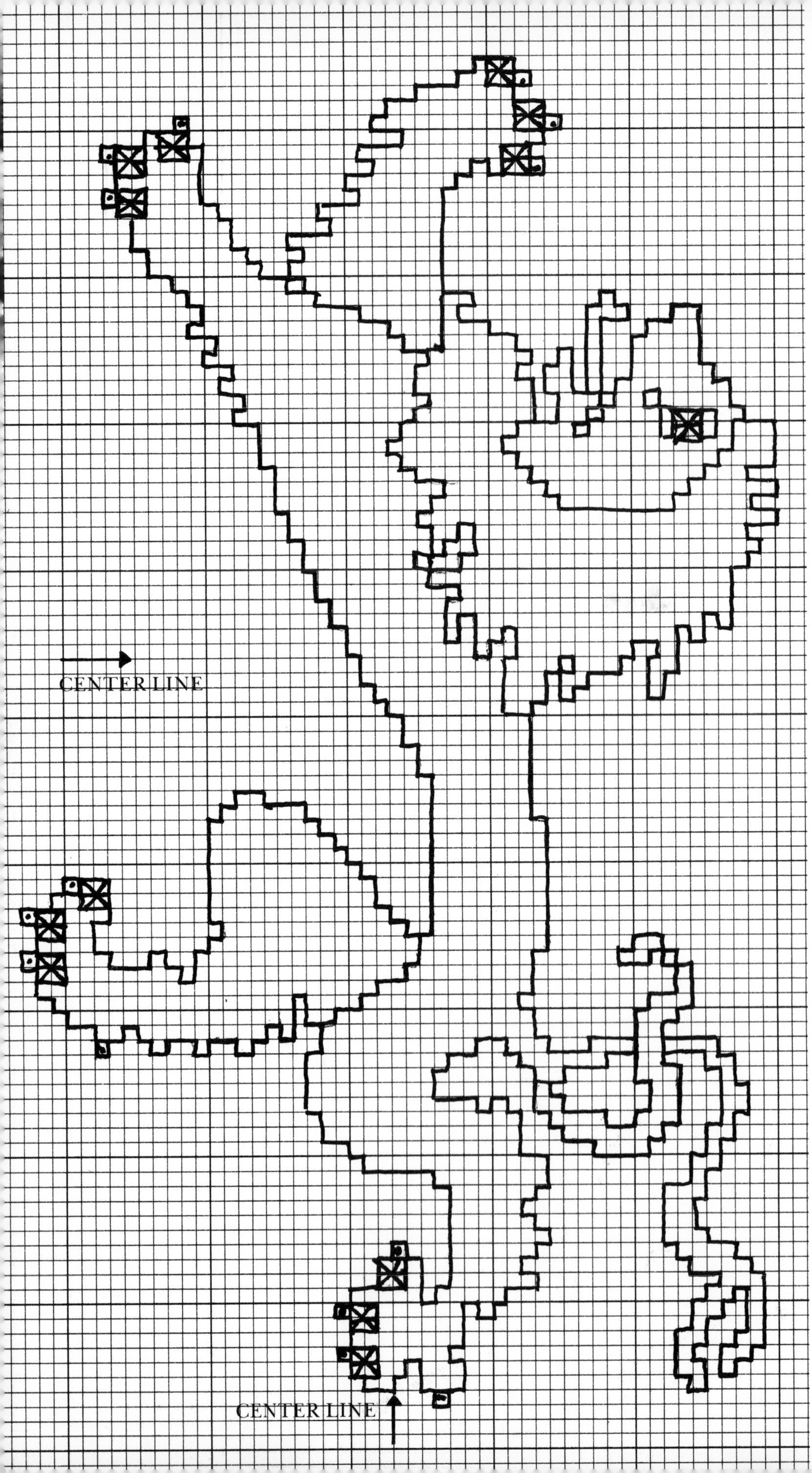

LION

CENTER LINE

CENTER LINE

LION

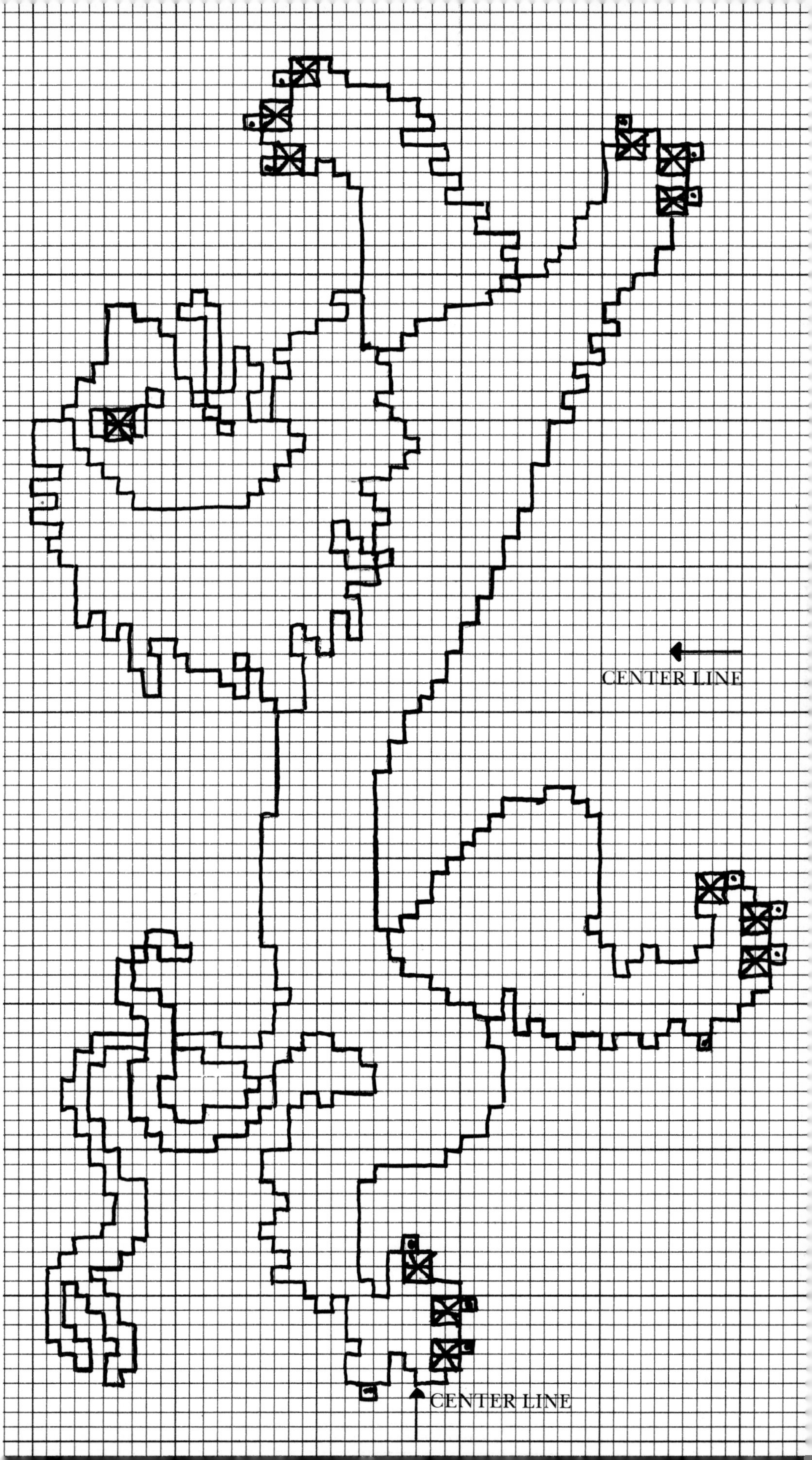

CENTER LINE

CENTER LINE

CALICO CAT (Miss Vee Footstool)

A word about Miss Vee: she is certainly the most charming *calico* cat I have ever met. I qualify the type of cat because my own black and whites, Tom and Jack, may take offense. Miss Vee lives in a penthouse in New York City with two other cats — Bête Noire and C 2. Their needs are met by the playwright Elinor Jones. There is no way in the world she could be described as the owner of these cats — quite the reverse. A portrait of Miss Vee done in needlepoint appears in color plate 18. While the portrait pillow was executed in realistic Vee colors, the graphed design here is for a calico cat of a more fantastic breed. Though if you knew Miss Vee, you would wonder how that could be possible.

I have kept the graph in outline form in case you want to render the design as a portrait of your own cat, or one of your acquaintance.

If you elect to stitch the piece as shown, however, here are suggestions for working:

The piece as pictured in color plate 17 is worked on #10 mono canvas.

The thread count of the top of the piece (excluding boxing) is 139 by 139. If you wish boxing on the piece, add 31 threads *on each of the four sides of the canvas.*

Persian yarn in white 005, blues 365 (darkest), 334, 386, 385, and 395 (lightest) were used.

The animal itself is worked in tent stitch.

The cushion on which she rests is worked in a Florentine stitch chevron pattern 4-1 step combined with the 2-1 step. The color is blue 385. The decorative stitches on the boxing of the cat's cushion are Algerian eyelets, again in blue 385. The background of the boxing is white 005, worked in tent stitch.

The ball fringe on the bottom edge of the cushion (the cat's) is made with a double Leviathan stitch, blue 385, with tent stitches of the same color on three sides of the Leviathan stitch. The tent stitch background of the entire piece is white 005.

To work the cat:

Work the face area first. Outline the area of the face from the ears downward in blue 330. Outline the eyes in blue 365. Stitch the pupils of the eyes in blue 330. Fill in with white.

The "v" shape between the ears and continuing down to make the nose is blue 395. The crown of the head is blue 386, except for the three "fret" lines, which are blue 365.

The largest area of the ears is blue 395; the lines outlining the ears near the forehead are blue 330. A few blocks on the graph at the base of the ears are dotted. These are worked in blue 334.

The tip of the nose is blue 334, the mouth line 365, as are the whiskers. The area to the right and left and the nose is white 005, as is the chin.

Outline the body of the cat with blue 365. The lines on the graph indicate the hip, folded front paws, and the body. Outline these with blue 365. Fill in areas with repeat patterns given in this chapter (page 141) if you wish, or decorative stitches of your choosing.

If you choose to add boxing for a footstool or boxed pillow, add the 31 threads to each of the four sides. Count off 31 threads at each corner, mark them, but do not work them. For mounting as a footstool, see Chapter VII, page 150. The boxing may be worked with repeat patterns as used on the body of the cat.

CALICO CAT

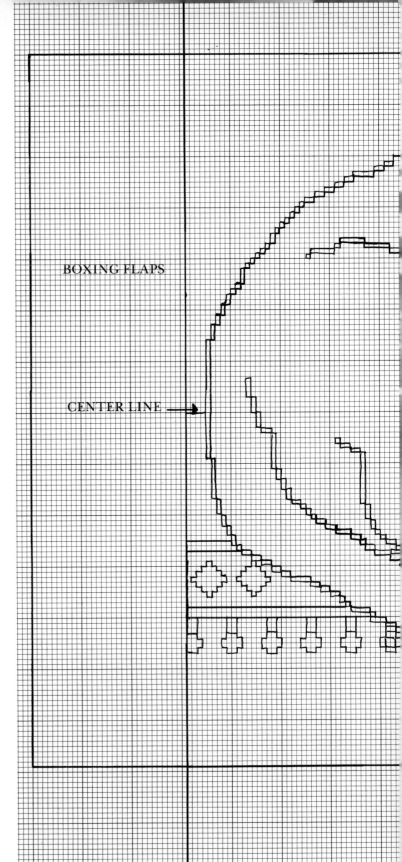

BOXING FLAPS

CENTER LINE ——▶

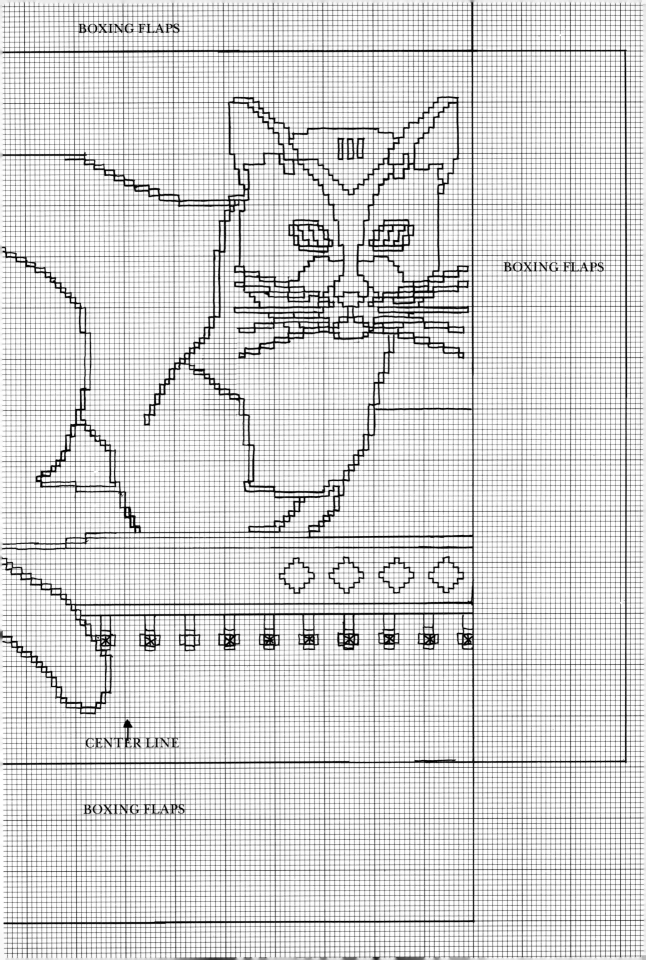

BOXING FLAPS

BOXING FLAPS

BOXING FLAPS

CENTER LINE

ORIENTAL CARPET SQUARE

(COLOR PLATE 9)

The sample piece is worked entirely in tent stitch on #10 mono canvas. The thread count is 173 by 173.

    Colors of Persian yarn used: red 952, medium red 962, light red 972; blue 330, black 105, and white 010.

Suggestions for working:

    The dotted blocks on the graph are to be worked in black 105. *All*

elements making up the design of the piece will then be outlined by that black. While the outlines for the motifs may be worked first, this can become tedious. I will assume that you will outline as you work, beginning at the center of the design, and no further instructions for outlining the individual components will be necessary.

In the small square in the center of the design are eight triangles, four to be filled with red 952, four with light red 972, alternating the colors. The narrow border surrounding the square is filled in with white 010. The small squares just inside the larger square surrounded by "hooks" are filled in with blue 330. The hooks and the narrow border from which they spring are filled in with white 010. Background of the area containing the small blue squares is red 952.

The triangles in the corners of the largest square have a series of triangles along the diagonal edges facing the hooks. These are filled in with blue 330.

The outside border of the triangle is light red 972. Surrounding the diagonal stripes inside the triangle is a single line of white 010. The stripes are alternating colors of red 952 and medium red 962.

A single line of red 962 is stitched around the large square. 962 is also the background color for the area between the hooks and the triangles. A border of two threads worked in blue 330 surrounds the square, followed by a single line of white 010. The stars are worked in alternating colors of blue 330 and red 962. The background of the star border is red 952. A single line of black 105 is worked around the square, making up the completed design.

ORIENTAL CARPET SQUARE

¼ OF DESIGN
to continue, turn graph ¼ turn to right

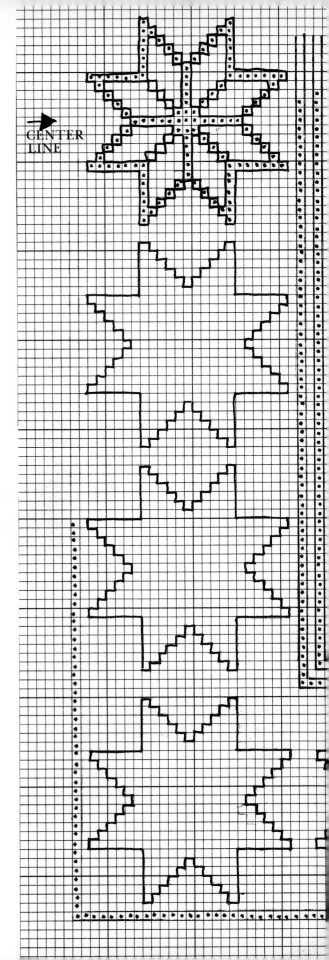

CENTER
LINE

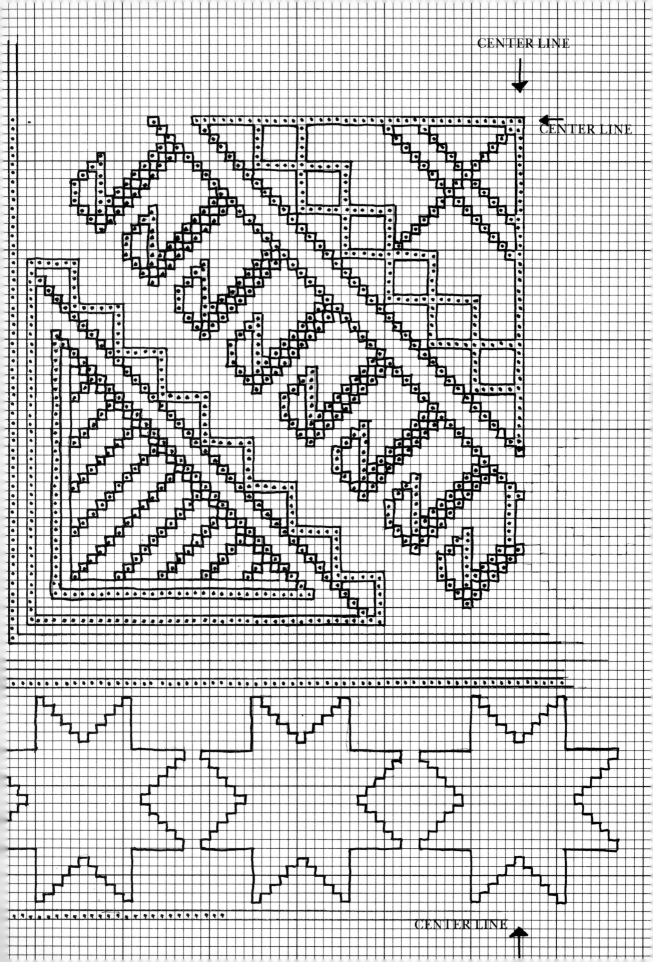

CENTER LINE

CENTER LINE

CENTER LINE

A small section of a graph using the stars as an allover design.

LATTICEWORK (COLOR PLATE 8)

The sample piece is worked on mono #10 canvas. Persian yarn was used in the following colors: red 952, blue 330, and cream 015.

The entire piece is worked in tent stitch. Thread count is 191 by 191.

Suggestions for working:

If you will work this design beginning at the lower right-hand corner and work toward your left, it will be simpler to follow. You will discover after you have stitched a complete unit of the design on the canvas that you will then not need to refer to the graph so frequently. However, I do not wish to mislead you: the design is very complicated. You may wish to color the design of the lattice with a drawing pencil on the graph itself. If this is done lightly, it will be readable and may be erased later.

The eternal knot, dotted on the graph, is worked in blue 330; the latticework in red 952; background color is cream 015, including the eight-thread border on the outside of the design. The square in the center may be worked in red 952 or in cream 015.

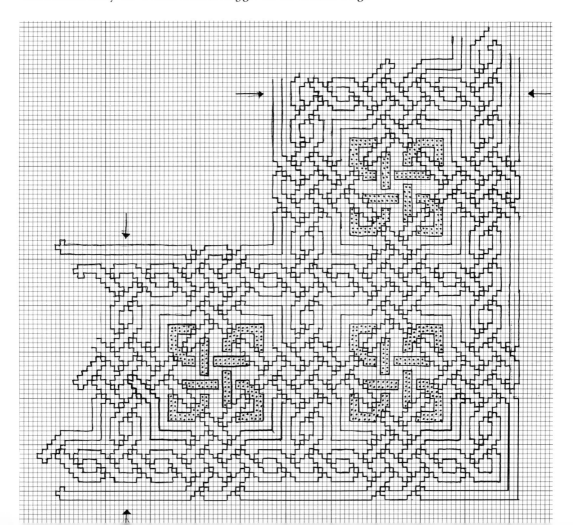

LATTICEWORK

¼ OF DESIGN
to continue, turn graph ¼ turn to right

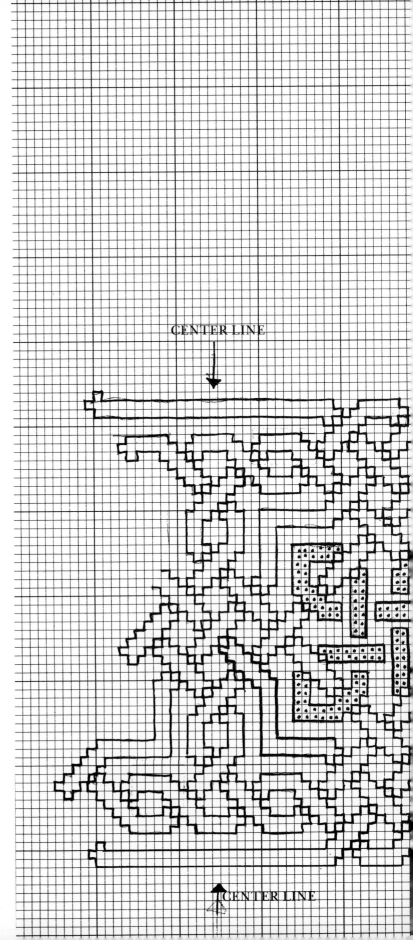

CENTER LINE

CENTER LINE

CENTER
LINE

CENTER LINE

WHIG ROSE OR LOVERS' KNOT

(COLOR PLATE 3)

This design was adapted from a woven coverlet design dating from the early eighteenth century. It may be used for a pillow as diagramed or, if the border is eliminated and the interlocking circles continued, it can be made as large as you wish for use as upholstery fabric.

The sample piece was worked on #10 mono canvas, using the tent stitch. The thread count is 151 by 151. Full strands of Persian yarn were used in the following colors: red 952, white 005, blue 365.

Suggestions for working:

Areas to be worked in red 952 are indicated on the graph by dotted blocks. The lines and squares forming the basic design of interlocking circles are worked in blue 365. The background is white 005. The border is worked in blue 365 and white 005.

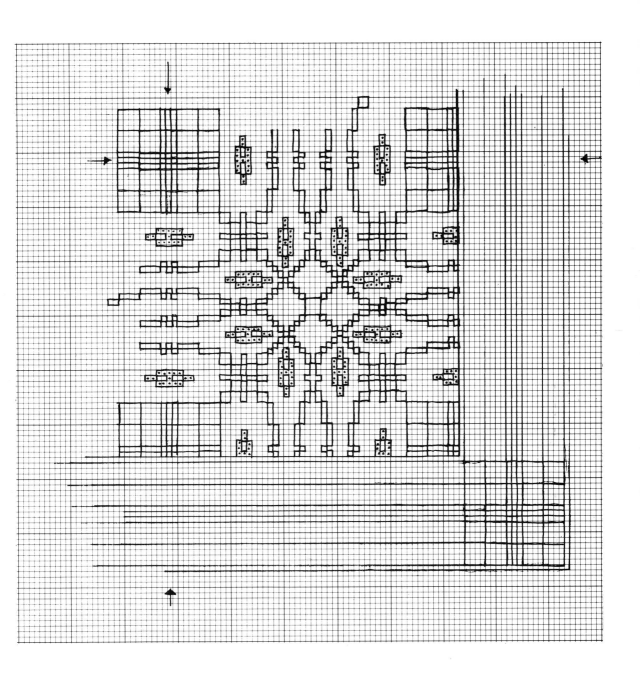

WHIG ROSE or LOVERS' KNOT

¼ OF DESIGN
to continue, turn graph ¼ turn to right

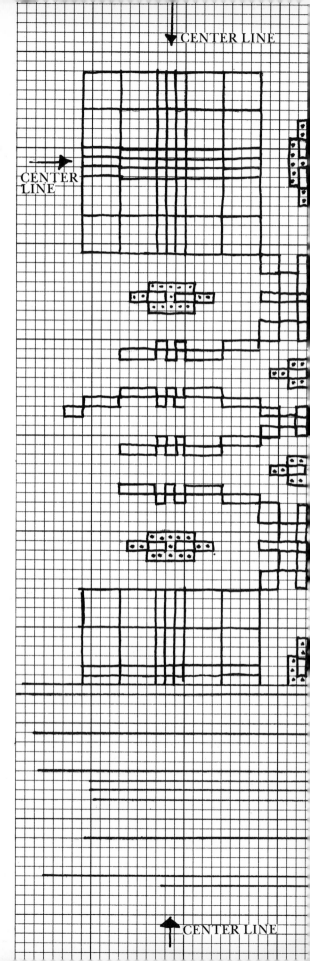

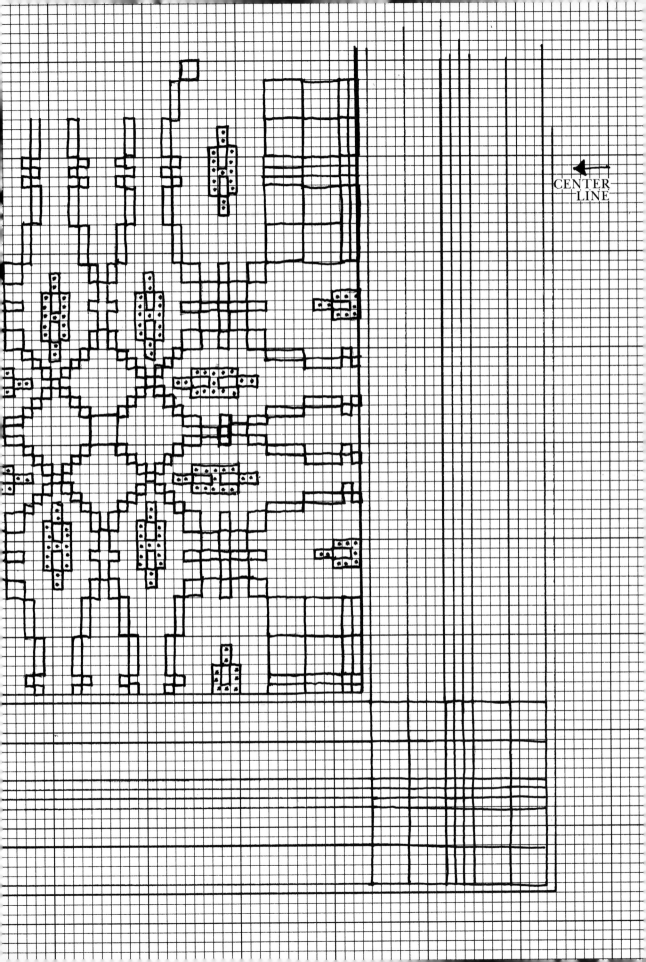

CENTER
LINE

QUAIL (COLOR PLATE 10)

I have included two graphs for the quail: one with the bird facing right, the other with it facing left. This is because of my generous nature and also because I want to make a pair of pillows someday with these quail facing each other from opposite ends of a love seat.

The sample piece is worked on #10 mono canvas. The area from the circle inward is worked in tent stitch; the background is worked in the brick stitch over two threads. The thread count of the design, including the circle, is 99 wide by 100 high.

The chair seat is worked with Persian yarn in the following colors: red 952, blue 334, cream 015, camel 466, brown 145, and black 105.

Suggestions for working:

Work the bill in black 105.

The eye is a single stitch of black surrounded with 8 stitches of brown 145.

The throat area is worked in brown 145. The small area separating the throat from the head and breast is worked in cream 015, as is the small space between the eye and the bill.

The head, crown feathers, and breast are worked in blue 334. The long narrow space along the back of the quail is worked in brown 145. Dotted lines on the graph indicate sharply defined feathered areas and should be worked in brown 145. These areas are filled in with cream 015 in the upper five sections; camel 466 in the lower. The lower portion of the breast is "tweeded": a single strand of white 015 mixed with two strands of camel 466. Feet and legs of the quail are worked in black 105. The circle is outlined and filled in with cream 015.

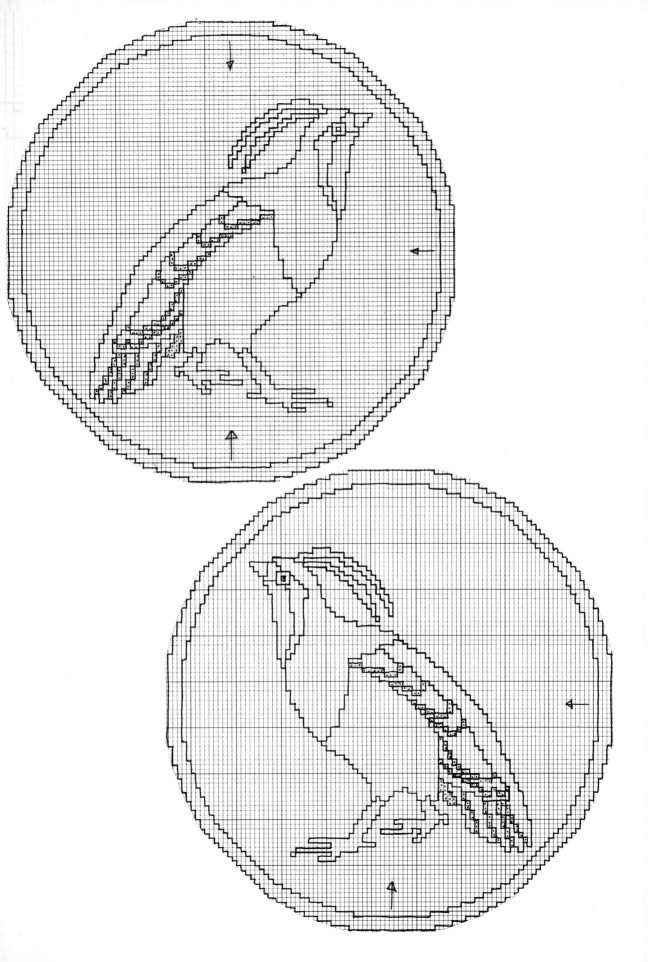

QUAIL

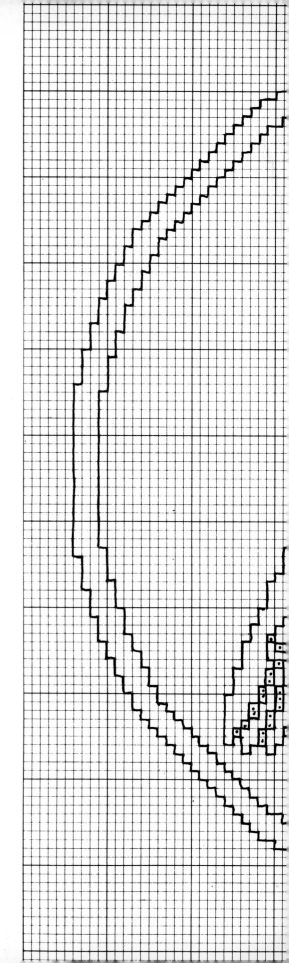

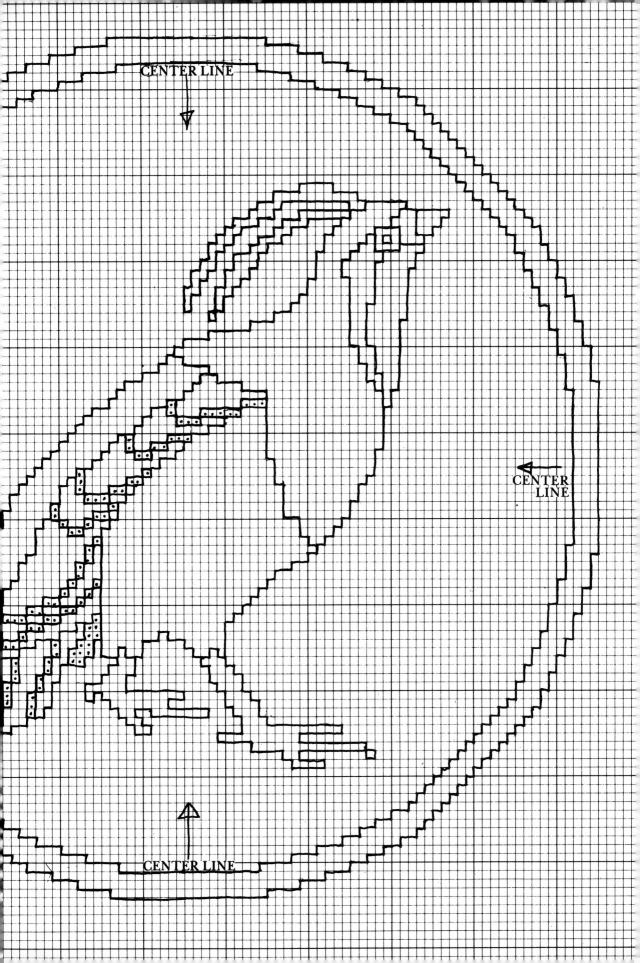

CENTER LINE

CENTER LINE

CENTER LINE

QUAIL

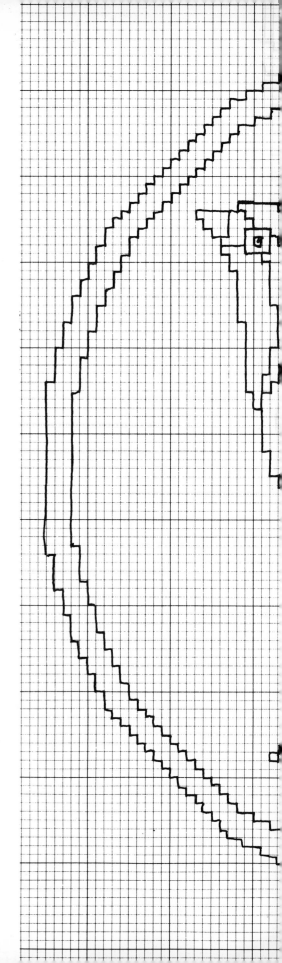

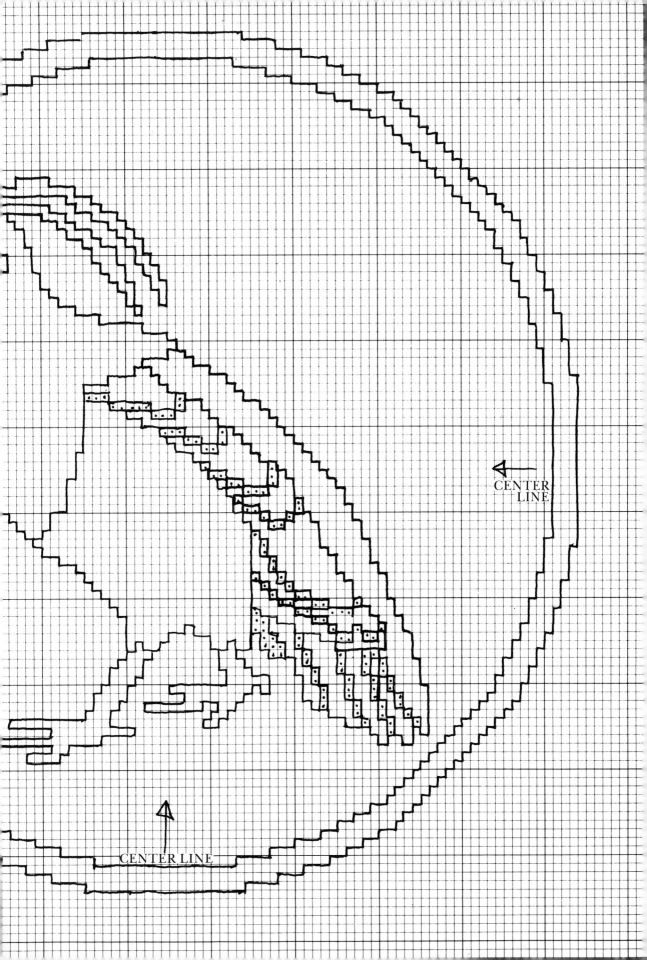

CENTER
LINE

CENTER LINE

ROOSTER (COLOR PLATE 13)

The rooster in the sample footstool is worked on #12 mono canvas. Thread count is 146 by 120.

Suggestions for working:

The background is worked in Persian yarn beige 496, using the brick stitch over two threads and worked horizontally. DMC six-strand embroidery cotton in the following colors are used for other areas: red 349, dark rust 918, medium rust 921, pale orange 402; gray 645, 647; green 472; blue 930. Four tent stitches of gold form the bird's eye, a piece of Persian yarn 440.

The major part of the bird's body (not the tail feathers) is worked in tent stitch.

The beak is worked in rust 918; area above the eye is pale gray 647; comb and wattle are red 349. A line of DMC black is just under the eye; below that is gray 645.

Outline the head, neck, wing, and breast of the rooster in dark rust 918. The neck feathers and those trailing onto the breast are filled in with rust 918. The breast and lines trailing onto the wing are medium rust 921. The rest of the wing is filled in with pale orange 402. The narrow strip just under the breast and continuing down to form the thigh is filled in with rust 918.

The feet and legs of the bird are gray 645.

Outline the tail feathers, using blue 930. The tail feathers are filled in with the Jacquard stitch, the uppermost area using blue 930 for the larger stitches, green 472 for the smaller. The next section of tail feathers reverses the colors, the third section returns to the original scheme. A small wedge-shaped area separates the next feathered area from the last; it is filled with green 472, using the tent stitch. The next, the smallest tail-feather area, is worked with green as the dominant color. Another small area just between the wing and the last tail feather worked is filled with tent stitches in blue 930.

The area just under the wing is in Florentine stitch, 4-1 step, worked in blue 930 alternating with the same stitch worked in the 2-1 step in green 472.

If you use a brick stitch background with this design, work a single row of tent stitch in the background color completely around the rooster design. Also fill in small areas with the tent stitch, such as the peaks of the rooster's comb, between the beak, and so on.

PLATE 1   THE CARNATION REPEAT

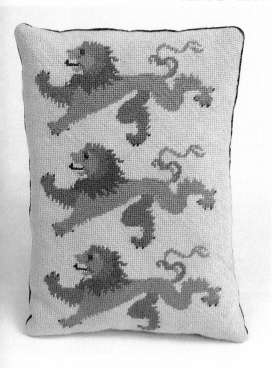

PLATE 2 LION

PLATE 3 WHIG ROSE OR LOVERS' KNOT

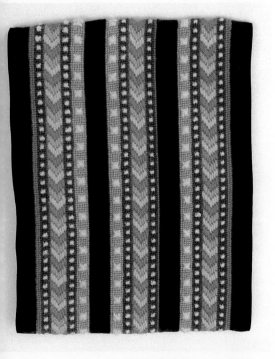

PLATE 4 THE RIBBON REPEAT

PLATE 5 BEE AND ROSETTE

PLATE 6 · THE FLAMESTITCH REPEAT

PLATE 8   LATTICEWORK

PLATE 7   PATTERNED STRIPES

PLATE 9   ORIENTAL CARPET SQUARE

PLATE 10   QUAIL

PLATE 11   THE PERSIAN MEDALLION

PLATE 12   THE SAW-TOOTH REPEAT

PLATE 14
BASKET WITH CHRYSANTHEMUMS

PLATE 13　ROOSTER

PLATE 15　SUNFLOWER

PLATE 16　COCKATOO

PLATE 17   CALICO CAT   PLATE 18   A PORTRAIT OF MISS VEE

PLATE 19   EMPIRE SWANS   PLATE 20   SWAN

ROOSTER

CENTER
LINE

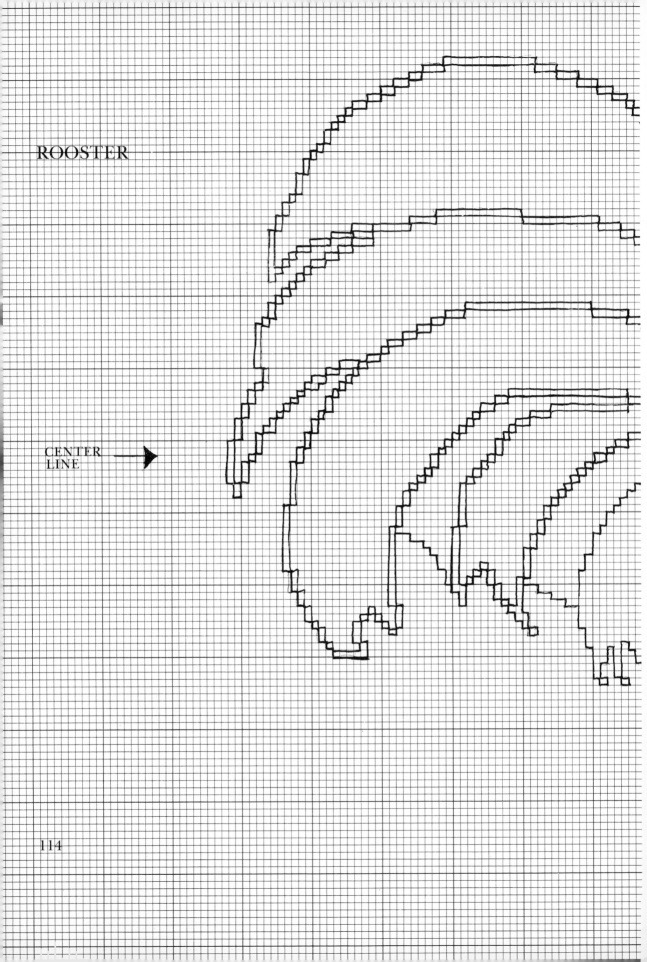

CENTER
LINE

CENTER LINE

COCKATOO (COLOR PLATE 16)

The sample of the cockatoo was worked on mono #14 canvas.

The thread count of the cockatoo itself is 185 by 85. Persian yarn in blue 365 and medium blue 330 is used for the beak, eye, and branch. The cockatoo's body uses DMC pearl cotton in white and yellow 973

Suggestions for working:

Outline all feathered areas of the bird's body with white pearl cotton. Outline the dotted area of the bird's crest with yellow.

The center of the eye is worked in blue 365, using the tent stitch, as are the beak and claws. The branch is in tent stitch blue 330. The eye is surrounded with tent stitch blue 330.

The dotted area on the graph, which you outlined on the canvas in yellow, should be filled with a decorative stitch in yellow. I used the leaf stitch, but you may choose from any of those stitches given in the Stitch section (Chapter IV).

The rest of the design may be filled with decorative stitches, using pearl cotton in white. Stitches used on the sample are Diamond eye, leaf, brick over two threads, half-eyelet, and the upright stitch over two threads. The last-named stitch is worked on the lowest tail feathers with the stitches laid horizontally on the canvas.

The background used on the sample is the double brick stitch over four threads in gold Persian yarn 441. The brick stitches are worked horizontally.

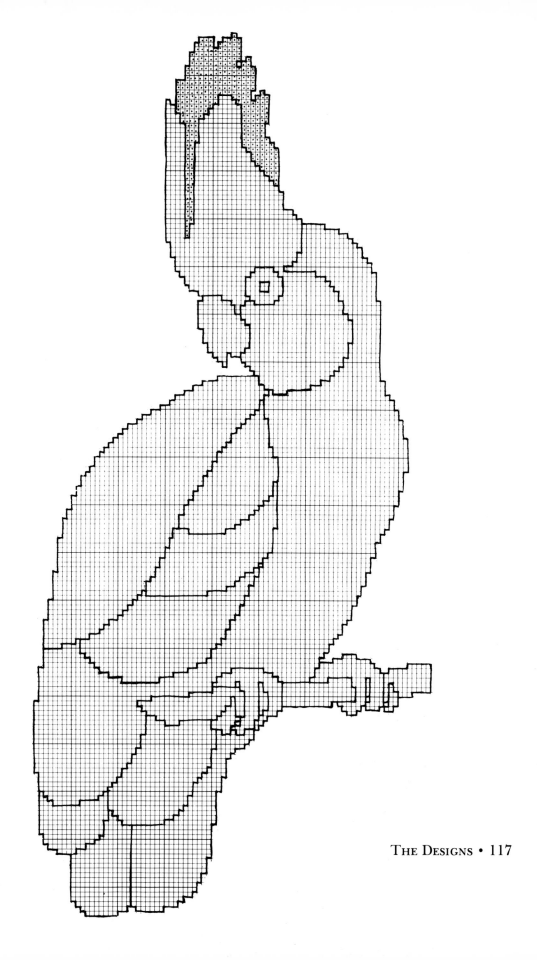

COCKATOO

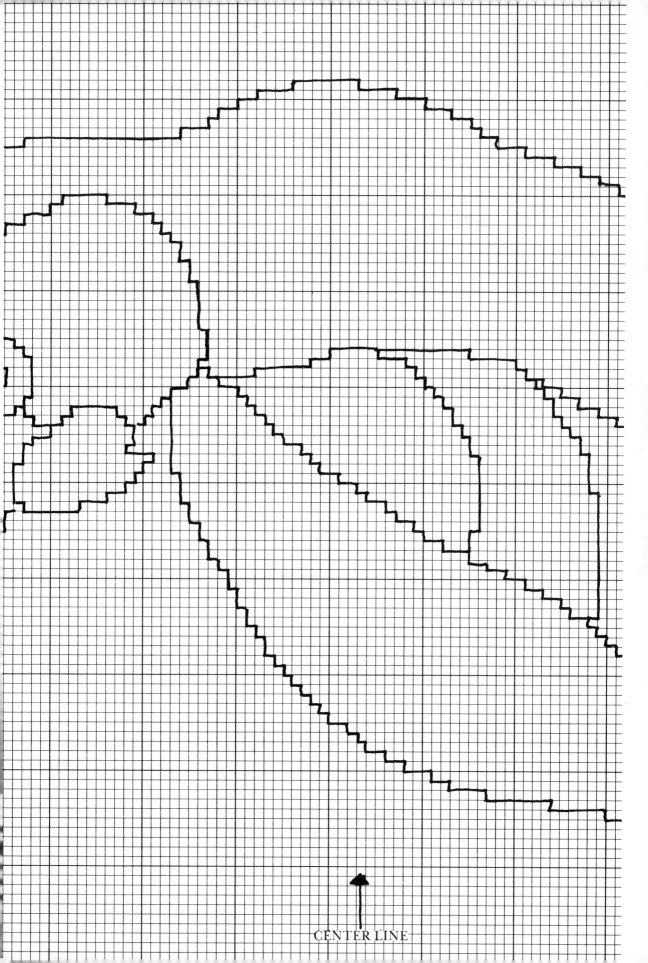

CENTER LINE

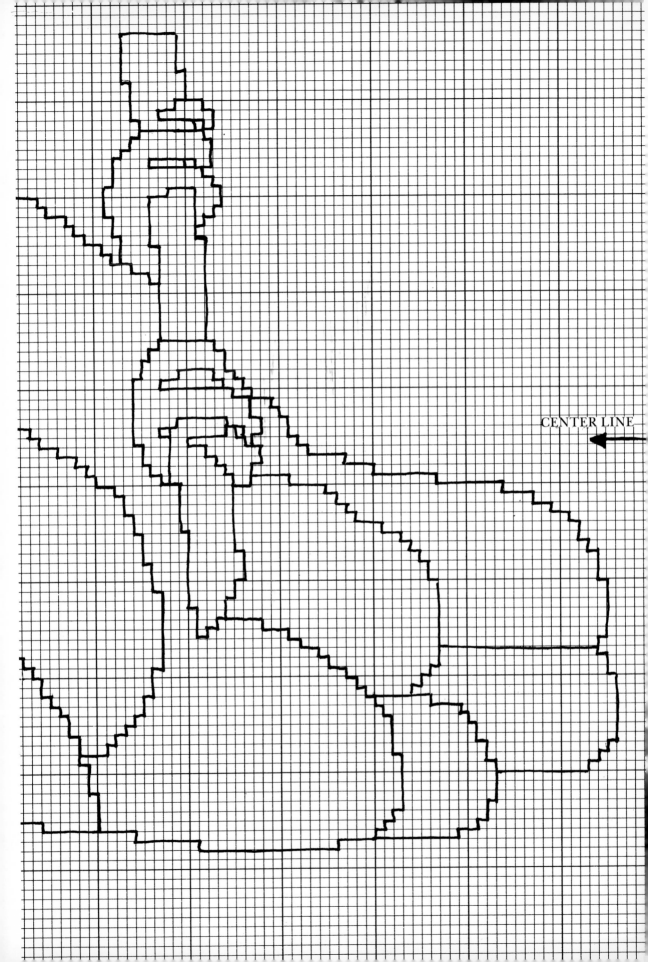

CENTER LINE

SWAN (COLOR PLATE 20)

Again I have chosen to give you a pair of graphs of birds so that you may, if you wish, work designs with the swans facing each other or away from each other.

The sample piece is worked on mono #12 canvas, using DMC six-strand embroidery cotton in the following colors: tan 640, beige 644, gray 3022, black, blue 336. The thread count of the swan itself is 108 by 69.

Suggestions for working:

Outline the swan's beak with beige 644, fill in with tent stitch. Make the two stitches forming the eye in black.

Fill in the small area just around the eye with gray 3022. The head of the swan is outlined and filled in with tent stitch, using tan 640. Outline the wing of the swan, using beige 644. Fill the entire wing area with leaf stitches worked horizontally, the tip of the leaf pointing toward the tail.

Outline the rest of the swan's body in beige 644. Fill the area just above the wing with tent stitch, using tan 640. The rest of the body is filled in with the rice stitch (crossed corners). The basic cross is stitched with tan 640, the corners crossed with beige 644.

The background is the diagonal tent stitch, using dark blue DMC 336.

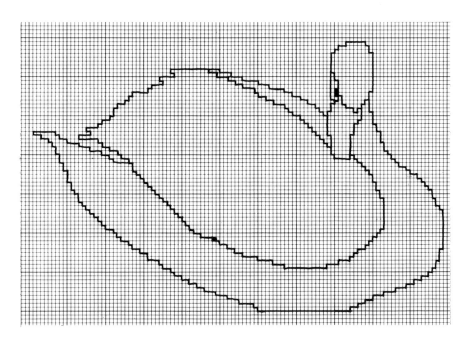

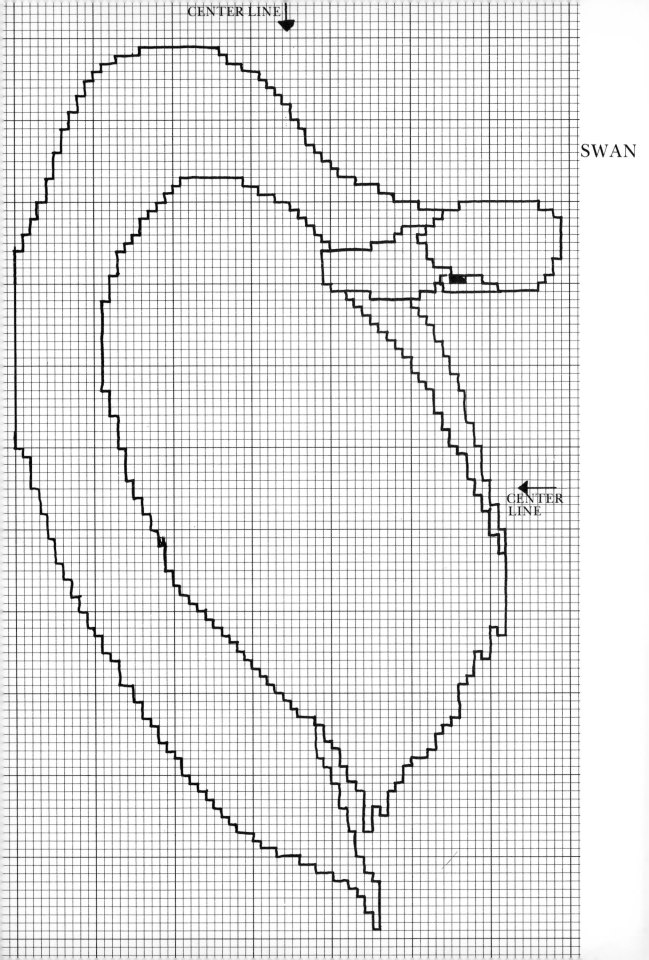

CENTER LINE

SWAN

CENTER
LINE

SWAN

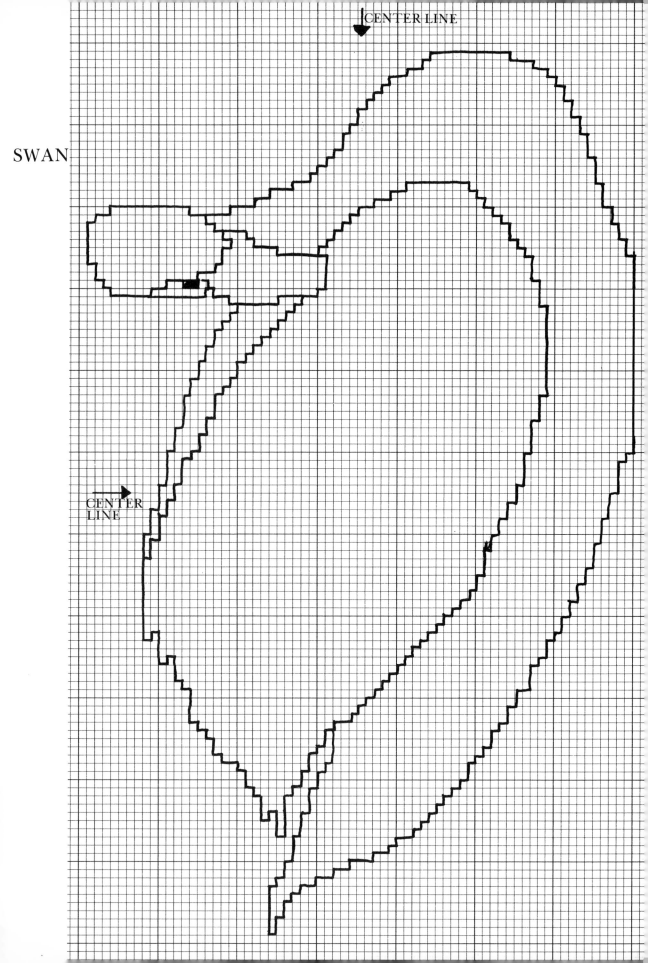

EMPIRE SWANS (COLOR PLATE 19)

The sample piece was worked on #12 mono canvas. The background was worked with Persian yarn brown 116. The rest of the panel was stitched with DMC six-strand embroidery cotton in the following colors: beige 644, tan 640, light rust 921, medium rust 920, dark rust 919, black.

The thread count is 110 by 260.

Suggestions for working:

Except for the wings of the two swans, the majority of the design is worked in tent stitch and should be used unless noted.

Work the two stitches of the pupil of the eye, using DMC black.

Outline the pupil using tan 644.

Work the beak using light rust 921.

Outline and fill in the neck and head with beige 644.

Work the scrolls on the breast with light rust 921.

Beginning at the top center of the design, outline the shape of the wing, using beige 644.

Outline and work the scrolled leaf at the bottom of the swan, using medium rust 922 for the leaf, dark rust 919 for the veins, which are dotted on the graph.

Complete the body below the wing by outlining and filling in the area with beige 644.

Fill in the front half of the wing, using a half-round eyelet stitch. The position of the first eyelet is indicated on the graph. End the eyelet stitches at the dotted line indicated on the wing.

Fill in the remainder of the wing with the leaf stitch, using beige 644. The position of the first leaf stitch is indicated on the graph.

Work the pearls and string in the swan's mouth. The pearls are beige 644, the string tan 640.

Work the same areas of the second swan in the same sequence suggested for the first.

Using medium rust 922, work the palm fronds in the center motif. The tips, shaded on the graph, are light rust 921. The small rosettes (three) located at the center top and left and right of center at the bottom are worked in beige 644. In the center of each rosette is one Smyrna cross-stitch worked in beige 644.

The center pole and small leaves are worked in beige 644, as is the decorative bracket binding the bottom of the palm fronds. The two-thread band on the bracket is medium rust 922, as are the two leaves at the very bottom of the center motif. The scrolls, dotted on the graph, are worked with dark rust 919.

The background of the sample piece was worked in the brick stitch over four threads whenever possible; in small areas, it was filled in with the tent stitch. If you choose to use the brick stitch for the background, first work a single row of the background color around every element of the design.

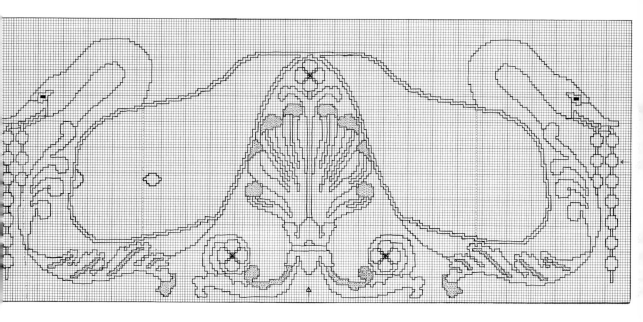

EMPIRE SWANS

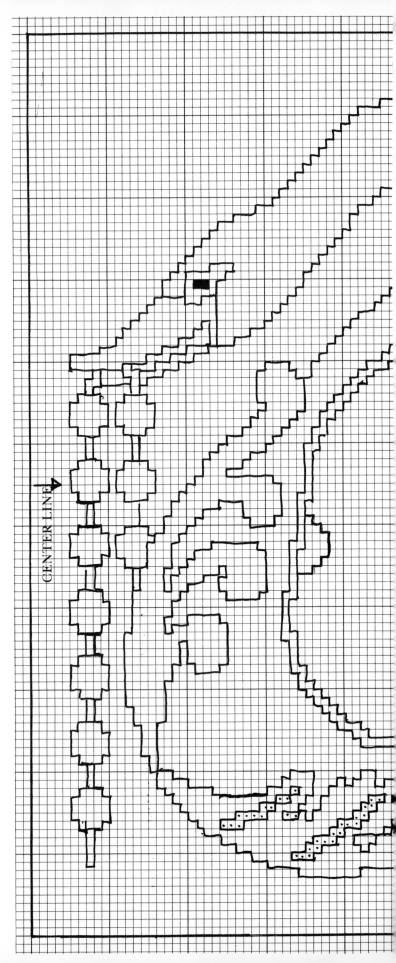

CENTER LINE

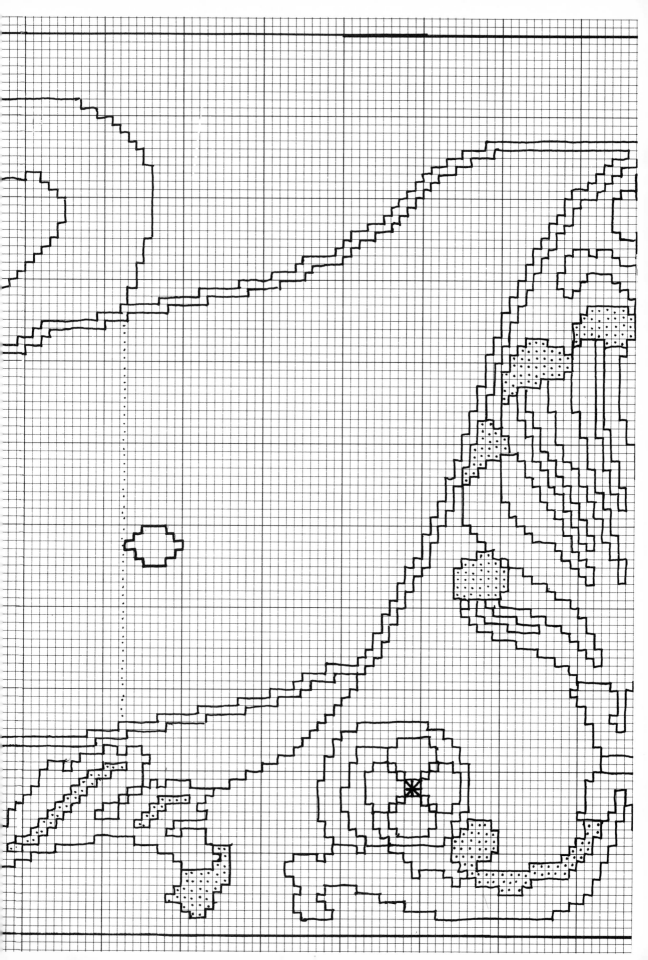

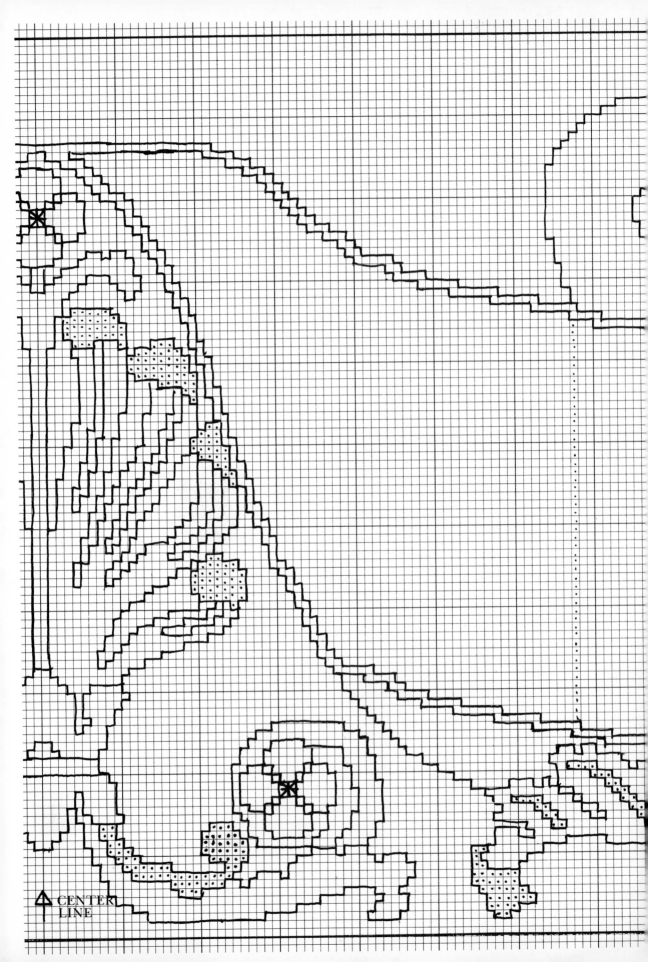

CENTER
LINE

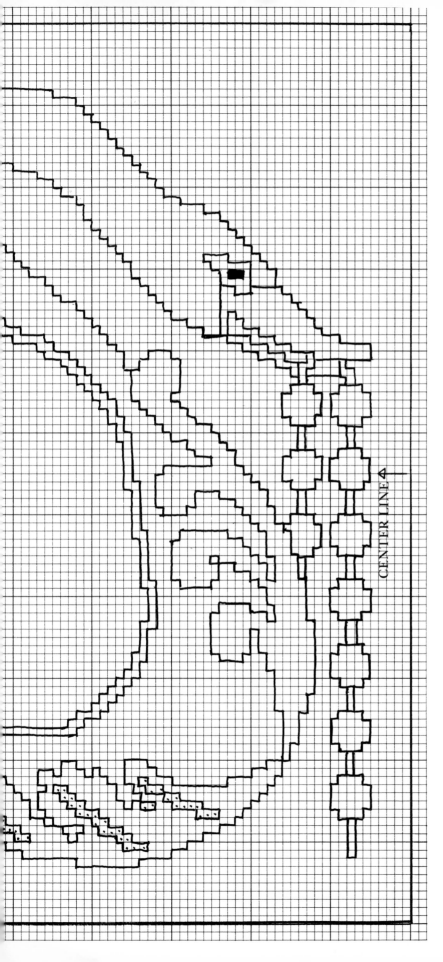

CENTER LINE

129

SUNFLOWER (COLOR PLATE 15)

The sample piece is worked on #10 mono canvas.

The thread count of the sunflower motif is 134 by 134.

Suggestions for working:

As the sunflower design is in fact a sampler, the color choice and the stitches are your preference. This would be a good design on which to use odds and ends of yarn colors and lengths. While the sample piece is worked in Persian yarn in gold, yellow, brown, and cream — thus the "sunflower" name — if worked in shades of red, pink, and white, it could be called the Poinsettia design.

However you choose to work the piece, first outline the petals of the flower. Fill the full petals with decorative stitches. The petals underneath full ones may be worked in tent stitch or filled with other stitches. The center may be filled with Smyrna or double Leviathan or even eyelet stitches.

The background of the sample was worked in tent stitch, though any background stitch may be used. The border added to the top of the square as photographed in color plate 15 is taken from the Ribbon Repeat design, page 76. The border on the boxing strip is taken from the Leaf and Bead design, page 78.

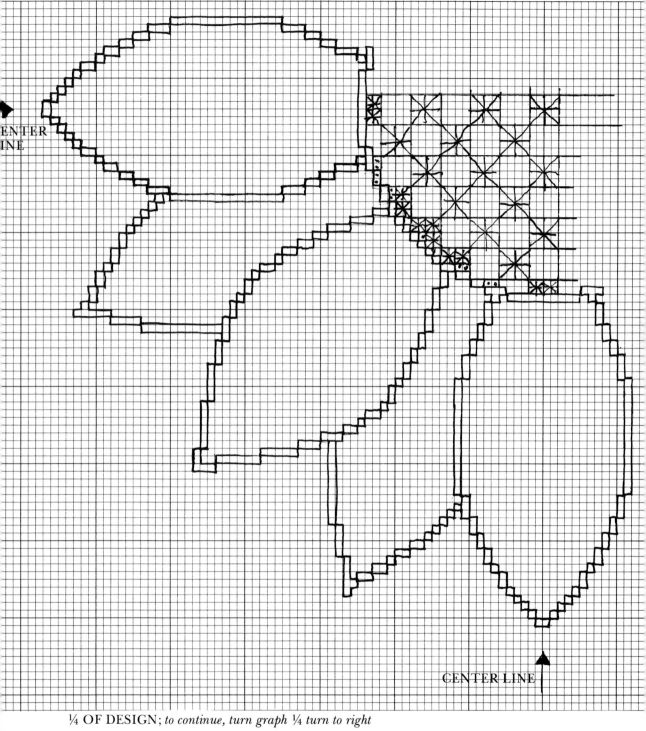

CENTER
LINE

CENTER LINE

¼ OF DESIGN; *to continue, turn graph ¼ turn to right*

BASKET WITH CHRYSANTHEMUMS

(COLOR PLATE 14)

The sample piece was worked on #10 mono canvas. Persian yarn was used for the piece in the following colors: blue 334, light blue 386; dark green 583, pale green 563. The flowers were worked in seven shades of gold: 427, the darkest, 440, 441, 442, 437, 438, and 040, the latter being the lightest. The thread count of the basket, flowers, and irregular background area is 120 by 120.

Suggestions for working:

The first two lines of the base of the basket are worked in tent stitch, using blue 334. The next two strips at the base are worked in the same blue, using the upright stitch over three threads. Using the Florentine stitch, 4-2 step, with blue 334, outline the sides of the basket. Outline the diamond shapes on the basket with blue 334. Still using the Florentine stitch, 4-2 step, fill in the diamond shapes with blue 386.

Before working the top rim of the basket, put in the flowers, using the ribbed wheel stitch. The centers of all the flowers are worked in the double Leviathan stitch or, if only a half flower, two Smyrna cross-stitches side by side. In all cases, the centers are worked in a color darker than the petals. For instance, when 427 (very dark gold) is used in the center, the next lighter tone is used for the petals, 440. If 440 makes the center, 441 is used for petals.

The small groups of double Leviathan and Smyrna cross-stitches are worked in the lighter tones.

Work the top rim of the basket in an upright stitch over four threads; the narrow band just below, over two threads. Use blue 334 for these.

Fill in the areas between flowers with tent stitch, using dark green 583. Work to the irregular line enclosing the flowers. If you wish to use the brick stitch over four threads as the rest of the background in the same color green, begin that stitching at this line. If you wish to change to a pale green (563), as in the sample, first work a single line of tent stitch around the outside of the dark green area only.

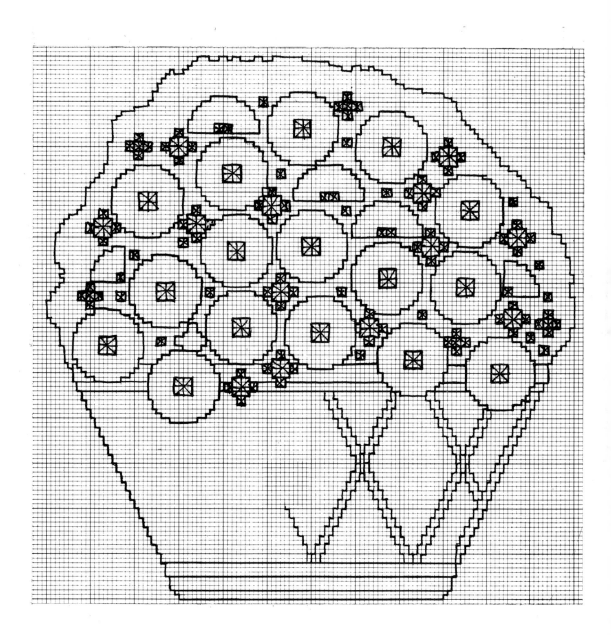

BASKET WITH
CHRYSANTHEMUMS

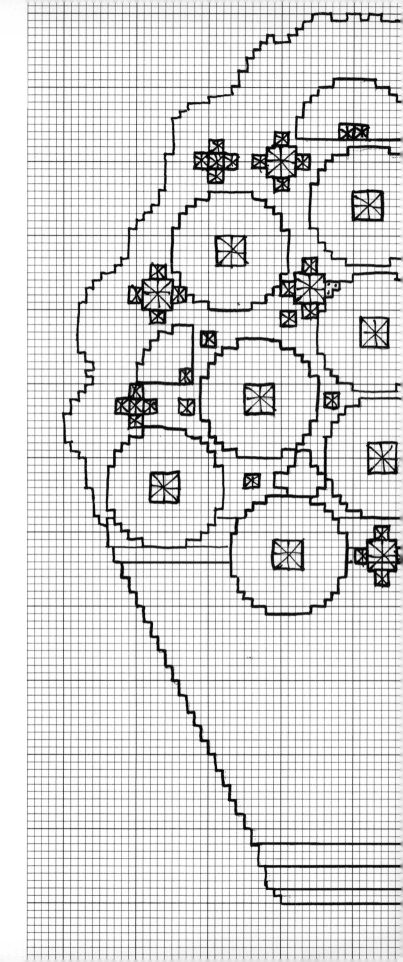

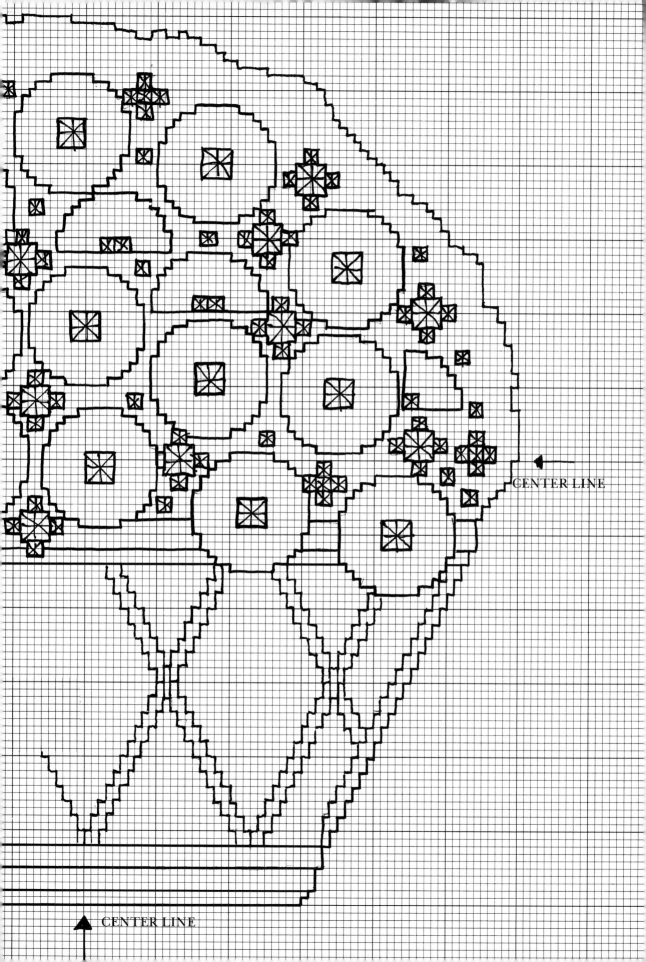

CENTER LINE

CENTER LINE

BEE AND ROSETTE (COLOR PLATE 5)

The sample piece is worked as a pillow on #10 mono canvas. The colors used are gold 447, brown 145, cream 015. All are Persian yarn. Gold metallic is also used on the piece.

The thread count, including boxing, is 211 by 211.

Suggestions for working:

(Except where noted, tent stitch is used throughout.)

The wings of the bees are outlined and worked in gold metallic.

The legs and feelers are stitched in brown 145.

The square forming the head is in brown 145.

The striped body alternates brown 145 and gold 447, the first stripe just below the head being gold.

The small motifs between the bees are stitched with gold metallic.

The background is worked in diagonal tent stitch, using cream 015.

The border of the top consists of four single lines of tent stitch and a double line of tent stitch at the outside edge. These are stitched in the following color sequence from the inside border to the outside edge: brown 145, cream 015, gold metallic, cream 015, yellow 447.

The stripes of the border at the top of the boxing use the same color sequence except that they are reversed.

The rosettes are stitched in tent stitch in yellow 447, the centers worked in gold metallic. Between the rosettes and next to the brown line of the border are Smyrna cross-stitches worked in metallic. The small lozenge shape centered between the rosettes is also worked with gold metallic.

BEE AND
ROSETTE

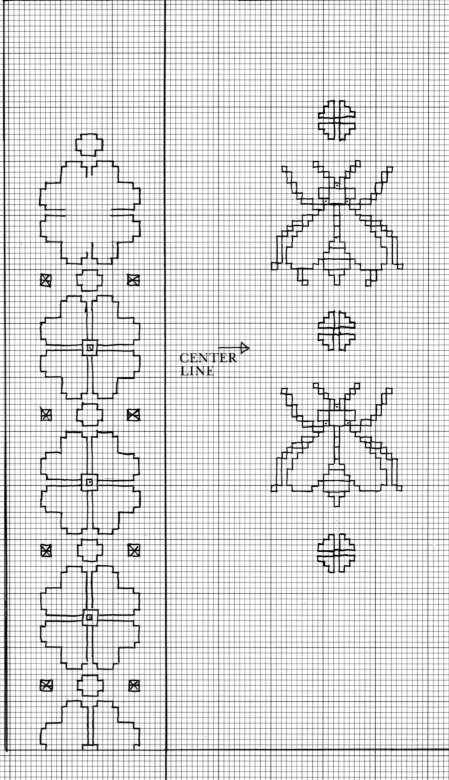

CENTER
LINE

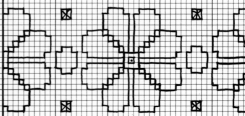

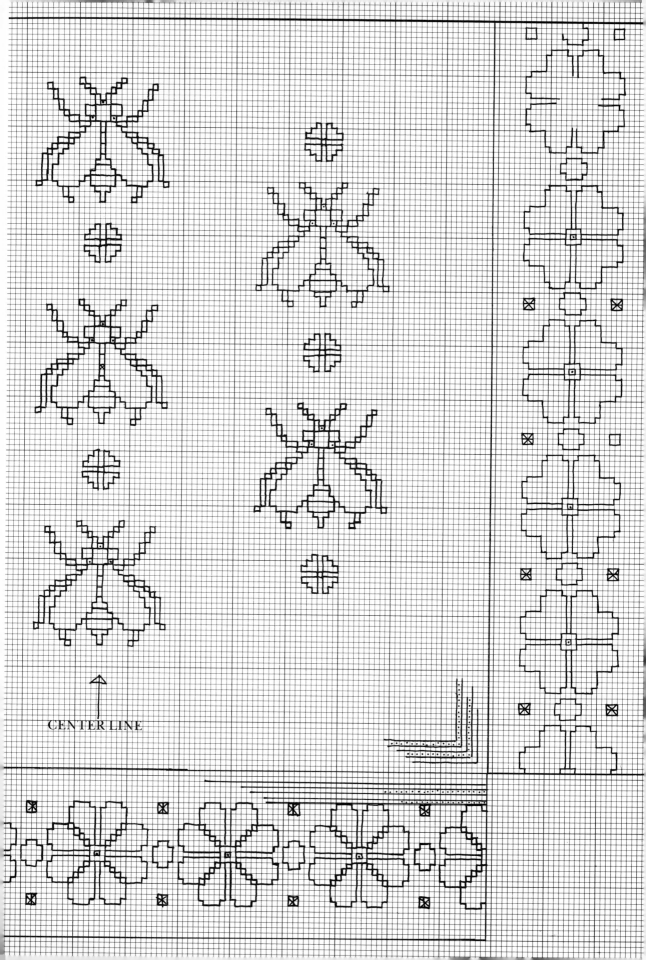

CENTER LINE

A striped pattern which may be repeated across your canvas.

140

REPEAT PATTERNS

Graphs of fourteen repeat patterns for you to use as you choose are included here. All of them are easily memorized after stitching them onto a small area of canvas and it will not be necessary to refer to the graph as often as with repeat patterns of more irregular design.

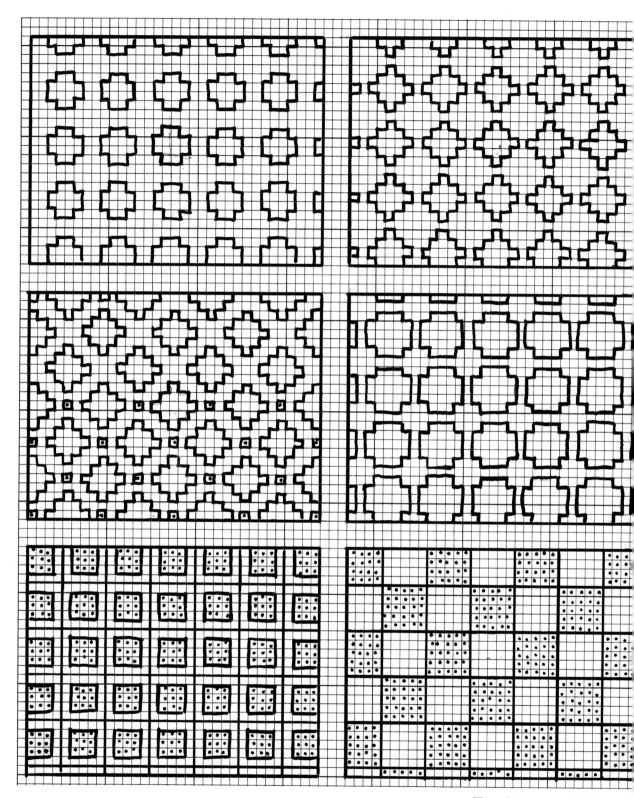

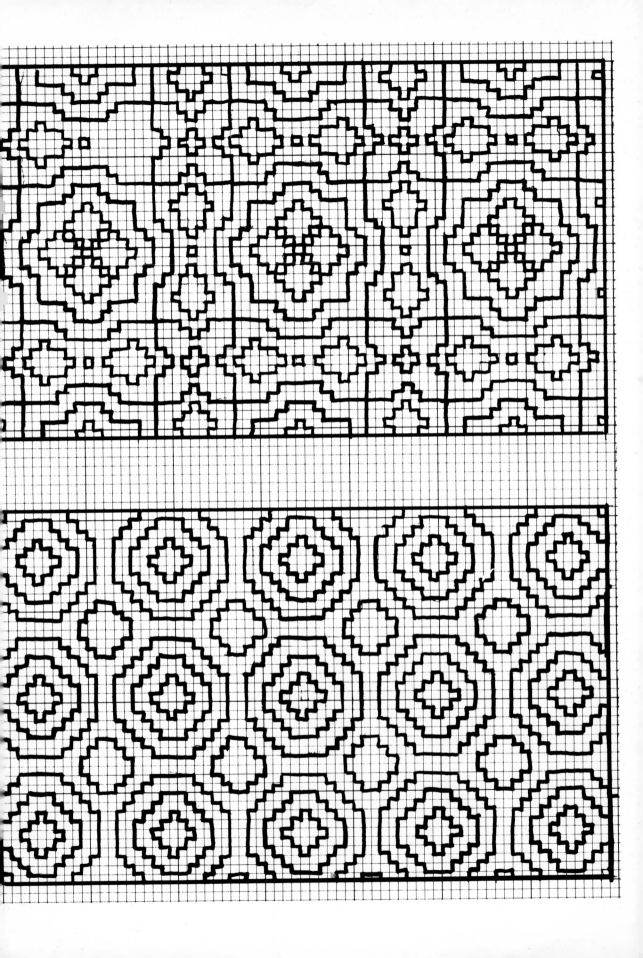

Chapter VI

Blocking the Needlepoint

EXPERIENCED needlepointers have passionate views about their own methods of working with canvas and yarn. There are those devoted to penelope canvas and won't have the other type in the house; some will work *only* with the continental tent stitch and loudly proclaim its virtues. Minor controversies exist in every area of the craft — including the blocking.

My particular approach to this necessary step in finishing a piece of canvas work is one of utter simplicity, yet requiring the most special kind of patience, perhaps, of the work.

Every piece of needlepoint will require some blocking to stretch it back into the shape and dimensions intended. Blocking the finished piece will also flatten the stitches to some extent and blend them into a smooth, albeit lightly textured, surface.

To block your own piece of needlepoint, you will need a few supplies, some of which you may have in your home.

The first item may have to be purchased: a piece of ¾" plywood. The size of the plywood should be determined not only by the needlepoint piece you plan to block now, but by possible future projects you have planned. A square of wood as small as 24" by 24" will serve for most pillows and other small pieces. The size of the

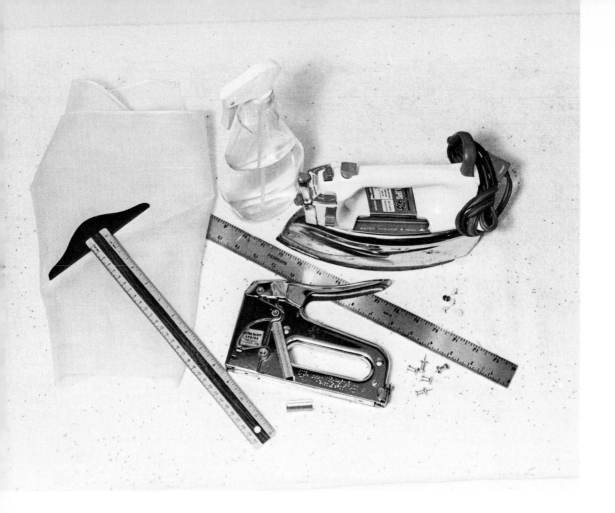

plywood in the photograph (here covered with toweling) is 24″ by 36″.

Regardless of the size, the plywood should be covered with a piece of fabric. An old blanket or a large towel will do just fine. I use the latter. Stretch the fabric over the front (smooth) side of the plywood; attach it to the back of the wood with tacks or staples. The fabric should be stretched so that there are no wrinkles.

An iron is necessary for the blocking process. It may be either the steam or the dry variety. I find a press cloth to be useful and prefer the see-through kind, which may be found in shops selling sewing supplies. A measuring device is also helpful. Cloth tapes are less desirable than a rigid ruler made of wood or aluminum. A T square is an optional tool, but it is helpful to use for squaring corners.

A spray bottle with water is necessary for my method of blocking. The one I use once held a liquid window cleaner, though one intended for spraying plant foliage will serve.

Something is needed to hold the canvas to the board. I find that a staple gun and 5/16″ staples are most suitable for the job. If you do not want to invest in such a tool, you may use aluminum push pins, thumbtacks, or rust-proof tacks.

The very first step in blocking your needlepoint is not to let anyone talk you into wetting the entire canvas. If you do soak the piece, not only will you have *great* difficulty in squaring it on the plywood; when the canvas has dried, it will be almost as stiff as that board.

Place the piece of needlepoint to be blocked *face down* onto the covered plywood; staple or tack it through the unworked canvas margin to the wood. Use the numbers as indicated on the diagram below as the sequence in which staples are placed.

The first side of the canvas attached (corner 1 to corner 2 on the diagram) should parallel a straight edge of the wood. You may measure from the edge of the plywood to the edge of the stitch at several intervals to be certain the side is straight.

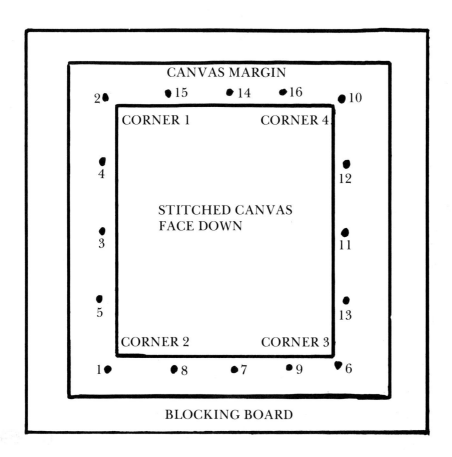

Make sure that corner 1 is "true" as in a square before you attach corner 3 permanently. A T square is helpful here.

Staple the second side of the canvas — corner 1 to 3; true corner 3 as you stretch corner 4 into shape.

Corner 4 may be more difficult to stretch than the other three. If so, spray the needlepoint *lightly* with water and it will be easier to manipulate.

Attach the remaining sides of the canvas — corner 3 to 4, corner 4 to 2 — to the board.

If the canvas is not squared to your satisfaction, remove the staples (use the blade of a screwdriver) on the two sides you attached last and redo them. Use a ruler to check the measurements of the stitched area. The measurements at the bottom should be the same in the middle, at the top, and in between those spots.

Never stretch the canvas *very tightly*. If you do, you will have a finished piece with (undesirable) scalloped edges.

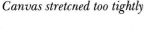
Canvas stretched too tightly

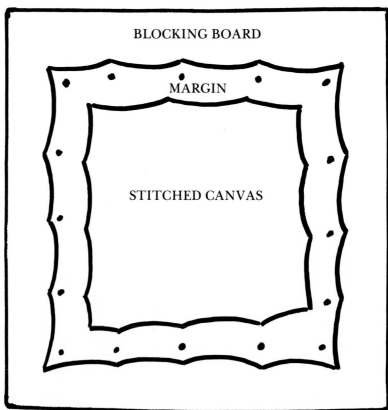

BLOCKING BOARD

MARGIN

STITCHED CANVAS

When the canvas is satisfactorily attached to the plywood, spray the piece (margins included) with water. Again, do not wet the canvas thoroughly; spray it so it will be damp to the touch. This process will be repeated several times during the blocking procedure; less water will be used each time.

Place the press cloth over the damp needlepoint. With the iron set at "Wool" or "Hot," press the piece thoroughly. Do not attempt to iron the canvas until it is dry, but rather press until steam from the canvas no longer rises.

Let the canvas alone for at least eight hours, then repeat the spraying (use less water), pressing, and allowing the canvas to dry.

On the *third* day, spray the piece very lightly with water, press thoroughly, making certain that every area of the canvas has been sprayed and pressed. Allow the piece to dry for another eight hours or so.

There are those who will tell you that the repetition of spraying and pressing is not necessary; that once-over-lightly is sufficient. If you follow *these* directions, you will then be able to visit those "once-over-lightly" folk and watch *their* needlepoint "drift" out of shape.

Remove the staples or tacks from the canvas and board and admire your blocked needlepoint. It is now ready to be mounted and used as you wish.

CHAPTER VII
Needlepoint on Furniture

A needlepoint design, when used to cover a chair, stool, bench, or sofa, strikes a one-of-a-kind note. While it is possible for you to stitch needlepoint coverings for every piece of furniture in your home, such a plethora tends to lessen this one-of-a-kind impact. One piece of furniture wearing needlepoint will possibly be the star of a room; several tend to become a chorus.

What to cover with needlepoint is not a knotty problem. Furniture stores and even some needlepoint shops have very handsome small stools, benches, and chairs that are easily covered with needlepoint, since the pieces are designed with wooden frames and slip seats. A slip seat is easily removed from the frame by removing the four (sometimes more) screws that hold it in place. These slip seats are usually covered in muslin and ready to receive a piece of worked canvas.

If you elect to cover one of these pieces with needlepoint, select the piece and measure the area to be covered before you begin to stitch. Work your canvas not only to the finished dimensions of the top, but add at least two inches of needlepointed canvas to each side for the turn-under.

The chair in the photograph is of a style I call Early Depression. It was found in a used-furniture store just as it is photographed, for less than three dollars. It is very sturdy and underneath its coat of

puce enamel is a core of solid oak. Someday the enamel will be stripped away and the seat will wear a needlepoint cover. For the purposes of this book, however, more enamel from a spray can was applied, this coat of royal blue. The seat was covered with needlepoint in the Quail design (page 106). The chair does now have a new lease on its life and might even be renamed in style: Early Uplift.

If you are planning to cover a large piece of furniture, such as a wing chair, sofa, or even a side chair with a "tight" seat (not removable), those pieces will require the services of a professional upholsterer. Before beginning work on the piece, consult with the upholsterer whom you wish to do the work. He will assist you with measurements and perhaps even supply you with a muslin pattern (or patterns) for the pieces you will need to work on canvas.

In your conference with the upholsterer be sure you get an estimate as to the cost of the work. A large piece such as a wing chair can cost several hundred dollars for the labor alone.

A further word of caution: select an upholsterer who has had experience in attaching needlepoint to furniture; ideally, one whose work with needlepoint you have seen.

Some of us seem to have an extra ingredient in the blood that flows through the veins: do-it-yourself. As I am one of those and hope some of you are, I am including *simple* instructions for making a stool to bear your needlepoint.

The only tools required to assemble this stool are a pair of pliers and a screwdriver.

The legs for your stool may be purchased in a wide variety of heights, styles, and finishes. They are available in hardware stores, home centers, and by mail from several places advertising these wares in home decorating magazines. Foam rubber is cut to size in upholstery shops, some fabric stores, and those shops selling only foam rubber. Plywood in a ¾″ thickness can be cut to your specifications at a lumber yard. The round-head stove bolts needed to attach the plates into which the legs screw are to be found in a hardware store. The diameter of the stove bolts will depend on the size of the holes you have drilled into the corners of the plywood; 5/16″ diameter is a good size.

Before assembling your own stool from the materials listed, the needlepoint must be already finished. It may be square, rectangular, or round. It must have a boxing — canvas or fabric. When the piece is completed, measure the top and make a note of the *exact* dimensions. Some canvases are woven with the horizontal threads slightly closer together than the upright threads. This can mean that your "square" top will measure slightly less on two sides.

After measuring the top of the piece, measure the depth of the boxing and add that measurement to your list.

Have the plywood cut to the same dimensions as the top of the needlepoint. Select foam rubber with a thickness the same as, or slightly thicker than, the depth of the boxing. Have the foam cut to the same size as the plywood.

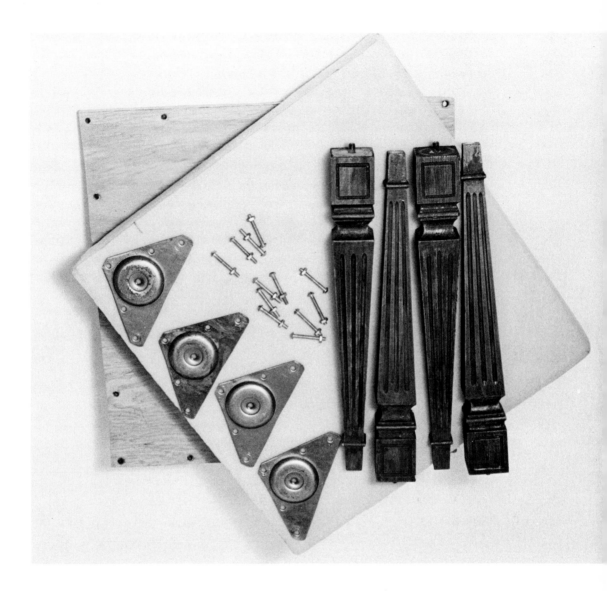

Attach the plates to the piece of plywood with the stove bolts, placing the round head of the bolt on the side of the plywood to be covered with the foam rubber. Secure the plates to the underside of the plywood with the nuts that have been supplied with the bolts. Use pliers to tighten the nuts and a screwdriver to hold the heads of the bolts if necessary.

Place the foam rubber on top of the plywood, screw the legs into position, and you are ready to place the needlepoint on the stool.

If you have stitched boxing flaps onto the canvas top, you will have left the corners unstitched. Bring each end of the boxing strips together at each corner, the unworked canvas square on the back side of the piece, and, using tapestry needle and yarn of an appropriate color, tent stitch the ends together.

Around the bottom edge of your (now) needlepoint "box," there will be at least a 2″ margin of unworked canvas. Fold this canvas to the back of the piece, leaving only ½″ of canvas below your last row of stitching.

Place the needlepoint on the just-made stool. Staple or tack the piece of unworked ½″ canvas to the ¾″ plywood thickness. Apply a piece of braid with glue or ornamental tacks to cover the staples, and your stool is ready for use.

CHAPTER VIII
Designing Your Own

As long as there are individuals responding to stimuli, there will be designs and variations of those designs. In its broadest sense — and the subject is *very* broad — design, to me, is an orderly arrangement of ideas.

Your life experiences will play a large role in your own designs. These experiences form your point of view. Monet's paintings of flowers are quite different from Brueghel's, as those of the latter differ from Picasso's or Matisse's. Yet all portray flowers and how the individual saw them.

Most people shy away from creating their own designs, dismissing the opportunity with "I can't draw a straight line." Graph paper and a straight-edged ruler can help you considerably if a straight line is what you want! And as we have seen on the graphed designs on these pages, straight lines, short and long, form the designs.

Before you put a design on graph paper, the design must be created or found. Books of designs abound in stores, libraries, and museums. Frequently a design can be traced directly from a book and transferred to graph paper. If this is not possible, it may be copied by an inexpensive photocopying process. If the design needs to be enlarged, this can be done by a shop specializing in enlargements and reductions by photostatic copying.

Large sheets of graph paper can be found in most stores specializing in artists' supplies. The usual size of the sheets, 17" by 22", which will accommodate a fairly large design, may be purchased singly or in pads of a hundred. Ask for blue-lined graph paper, 10 squares to the inch, cross-sectioned.

To put a design on the graph paper, either trace the line drawing onto the paper by placing the design underneath and holding paper and design up to a light (a windowpane is *very* good) or by laying an object, such as a leaf, plate, cut-out shape, or whatever your choice may be, directly on the face of the paper and tracing around it, using a soft-lead pencil.

After you have traced the outline, use the same pencil to "step" the design. You may see "stepping" graphically illustrated on any graph in this book. A good rule to follow in stepping the design is that if your drawn line occupies one-half or more of the small block through which it passes, that block should be included in the steps. If it occupies less than one-half of the block, it should not.

I feel very strongly that each needlepointer, after an apprenticeship with the tools and techniques of needlepoint, should express his or her own view in design. This apprenticeship may be brief, but in order to break rules one must know what the rules are. You can only break fresh ground after you learn what ground has been broken!

In the area of design — as in life — only YOU are YOU. Only you have amassed your particular experiences. You are unique in all of time. If you allow those experiences — pleasant *and* painful — to shape your viewpoint, your designs will be unique. You should *try*. Take your yearnings, urges, nostalgia, knowledge, and put them on canvas.

While your talent for drawing objects in a realistic style may be less than Holbein's, it *may* be greater than Grandma Moses's. Though their styles differ greatly, both artists put designs on *their* canvases that evoke emotion, appreciation, and express a point of view in an orderly arrangement.

stepping a design ▶

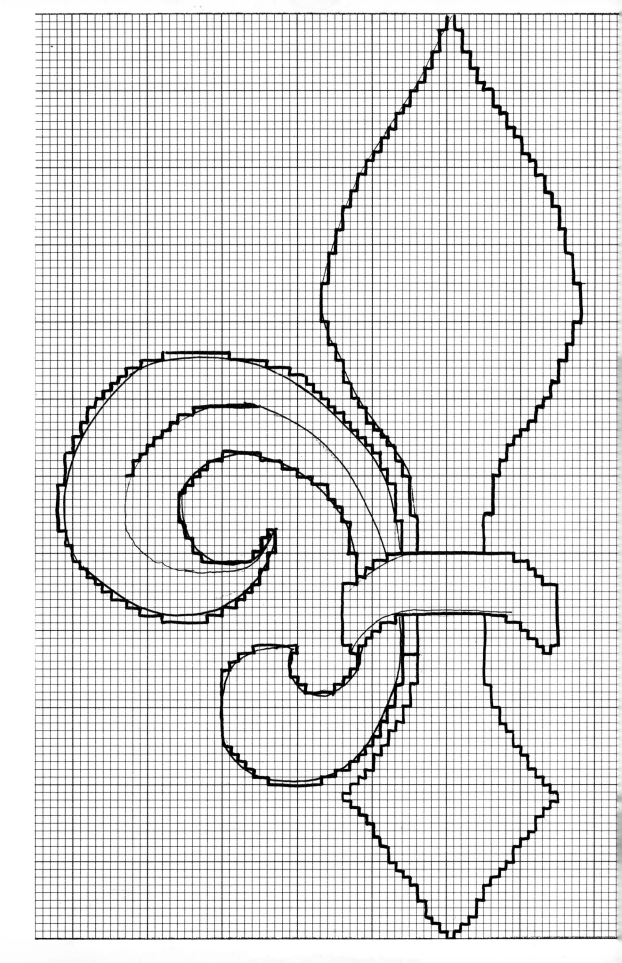

Bibliography

Dillmont, Thérèse de. *Encyclopedia of Needlework.* Rev. ed. France: Mulhouse, 1890.

Lane, Maggie. *Rugs and Wall Hangings.* New York: Charles Scribner's Sons, 1976.

Lantz, Sherlee and Lane, Maggie. *A Pageant of Pattern for Needlepoint Canvas.* New York: Atheneum, 1973.

Philp, Peter. *Furniture of the World.* New York: Galahad Books, 1974.

Rhodes, Mary. *Needlepoint, The Art of Canvas Embroidery.* London: Octopus Books, 1974.

Snook, Barbara. *Florentine Embroidery.* New York: Charles Scribner's Sons, 1967.